77 Ways to Get the Edge at Casino Poker

A Scoblete Get-the-Edge Guide

77 Ways to Get the Edge at Casino Poker

Playing and Beating the Best!

by Fred Renzey

Foreword by Frank Scoblete

Chicago and Los Angeles

06 05 04 03 02   5 4 3 2 1

Library of Congress Control Number: 2002104264
ISBN: 1-56625-174-5

Bonus Books
160 East Illinois Street
Chicago, Illinois 60611

Printed in the United States of America

To my dad, who died before I began to play poker as a serious, competitive game. I never understood his "strange," conservative/aggressive playing style. Now I do. I wish I could tell him so.

Table of Contents

Foreword

by Frank Scoblete

Poker is as American as apple pie and 4th of July fireworks. It is the quintessential home card game and the ultimate casino card game. Poker lore has entered our vocabulary ("The buck stops here." "Bluffing." "Playing them close to the vest." "Poker faced." "Four flusher.") and many politicians and teachers use poker analogies to push forth their agendas or lessons.

Just about everyone knows something about poker. Just about everyone has played some variation of the game, if only on their kitchen tables with their friends and relatives.

The first games of poker I ever played were with my cousins, when I was a kid. We played one penny–two penny. Almost everyone stayed in on almost every hand, no matter how bad the cards were running; and almost everybody raised everybody else, just to see the pots grow. And the pots were huge, sometimes 50¢ or more, and I usually won more money than most of my kin simply because I didn't go into every single pot—just most of them. We had almost no knowledge of the game or the odds or the psychology; we just knew this hand beat that hand and we could raise three times.

The little knowledge I had, which was infinitesimal, was enough to keep me out of the hopeless hands (we played a lot of 7 Card Stud and Jacks-or-Better Draw Poker) and give me a slight edge.

Of course, as I grew up, the games became bigger, 5¢/10¢, then 25¢/50¢, then $1/$2 in college. My poker circle, thankfully, was composed of essentially really bad to awful players, which allowed me to win small amounts of money from them on a regular basis. I did so not because I was good, but because I was less bad than they were. If you ever saw the movie *Rounders,* you might say I and my compatriots were *bounders.*

In the course of my gambling career since college, I have played in casino card rooms in both Vegas and Atlantic City. But the skills that allowed me to win in my youth (i.e., being less awful than the other players) just couldn't sustain me in the casino games. I was just terrible the first time I played in a card room...and the second time...and the third time. The other players ranged from bad to good—but they were all better than me!

Here is a truth to chew: Somewhere in America the worst doctor is practicing; somewhere the worst dentist is holding a drill in his hands; in some school the worst teacher stands amidst the rubble of paper airplanes, spitballs, and, in today's schools, God-knows-what else; in some courtroom the worst lawyer is arguing unpersuasively for his client and the worst judge is bringing his limited intellectual capacity to bear on something serious in the lives of other people. There is a worst major league baseball player and a worst fighter and a worst basketball pro. So the following statement should come as no surprise: At this very moment, at card tables in casinos all over the country (and, yes, the world), from high-limit games composed of professionals and seasoned amateurs to low-limit games composed of studious or instinctive players, someone is the worst player in that game. Some poor guy or gal is a sheep primed for a good fleecing.

Here's a frightening thought: At times the worst player at a game might even be you!

Enter Fred Renzey. Fred is not a good poker player; he is a terrific poker player; one who combines a deep mathematical knowledge of odds with good instincts for reading his fellow players. For years, he has been writing about poker for various magazines such as *Midwest Gaming and Travel* and *Poker Digest,* among others. Renzey is a true card sharp, an expert in both poker (a difficult game requiring insight) and blackjack (an easy game requiring rote memory). His blackjack book, *Blackjack Bluebook: The Right Stuff for the Serious Player*, is considered one of the best blackjack books on the market.

The book you are holding in your hands is not necessarily the key to fame and fortune at poker; but it is one key to helping you develop into the best possible poker player you can be. This book is not really for beginners but for those players who have played the various casino poker games and are looking to hone their skills—their *art* as Fred calls it. Whether you are an experienced amateur or an expert player, you'll find something to ponder in this book because this is really a book about *applied thinking* to the game of poker.

Divided into 77 "concepts"—some applicable to all games, some applicable to specific games—Fred will take you step-by-step through a process of thinking that will allow you to learn how to truly read your hand as it relates to an opponent's hand. The insights you'll gain from this book will be worth their weight in winning pots!

77 Ways to Get the Edge at Poker is not a book to be read in one sitting. Some books are made to be chewed thoroughly and digested slowly; this is one. You might want to take one concept per day and really explore it, examine it, hold it up to the light. Remember, no matter how good you are, or how good you think you are, there is always room for improvement. Indeed, today's poker players are getting better every day as more and more of them learn about pot odds and proper starting hands and the uses of check/raises and the bluff. Instinctive players, those who rely solely on their sense of things, are finding that the competition is getting fiercer.

The book you are holding will allow you to get into the mind of an extraordinary poker talent—without having to pay a serious price. It is much easier on you and your wallet to be educated by Mr. Renzey in the pages of this book first than to learn the same costly lessons from him across the table of your favorite card room!

Savor this book. It is a delicious poker meal.

Preface

With every other game in the casino, your adversary is the house. But in poker, other casino customers are your opposition. Does that make a difference? You bet it does!

You see, in most casino games the house gains the upper hand by simply handing you the short end of the proverbial gambling stick. It's a very basic principle. At roulette, for example, they'll pay you even money if you can guess whether the next color that comes up is either red or black. The problem is, there are only 18 reds but 20 non-reds, including the green 0 and 00. Yet, if you bet black you have the same deal, 20 non-blacks. The odds are always 20-18 against you—so they've got you coming and going.

Poker is different. In casino poker, the house doesn't play at all. It just supplies the table, the chips, the cards, and the dealer. The casino makes its money from poker by charging each player a "rake." That's either the money taken out of each pot, or an hourly charge for renting your seat. Either way, this rake constitutes an overhead which results in an initial disadvantage to the player. Fortunately, the game of poker involves such a high degree of skill that a good player can handily overcome that rake *by outplaying his opponents*!

In medium to higher stakes poker games, your rake will usually amount to 0.65 percent to 2 percent of your total betting action. That's your disadvantage going in. If you can play poker just 3 percent or 4 percent better than your opposition in these games, you've got the *edge*, and will make money over time. *In fact, many players do exactly that year in and year out!*

Another basic fact you should understand about public poker is this; as the stakes escalate, the rake *percentage* actually *shrinks*. In a low stakes $1–$5 Stud game, the pots are so small that the rake (usually $3 or $4 per pot) puts you at an 8 percent to 10 percent disadvantage!

By contrast, in a fairly high-stakes poker game such as $75/$150, players usually rent their seats for about $20 per hour. Playing solid poker, you'd put in about $3000 worth of action during a typical hour of play—making your overhead (disadvantage) just 0.65 percent ($3000 divided by $20)! At mid-range $15/$30 stakes the rake usually amounts to about 2 percent of your action—another beatable scenario. The higher you play, however, the tougher the opposition tends to get. So know your skill limitations and select your games carefully. Having gotten all that out on the table—let's get on with the business of learning to beat casino poker!

Orientation

The Structure of Casino Poker

The poker advice supplied throughout this book is aimed at *medium* to *upper* stakes games that have fixed limits. *No* limit and *pot* limit poker are games of a different ilk and will not be addressed. Most fixed-limit games are a two-tiered structure, such as $15/$30 (medium stakes), or $75/$150 (upper stakes). "Two tier" always means that no matter what the game, the first two betting rounds are for the lower amount and all the remaining rounds are for the higher amount.

All casino poker games are played "check or bet" and there doesn't necessarily have to be a bet made on every card. In addition, you may check, then raise if somebody else bets—a maneuver that might be frowned upon at your local VFW hall.

STUD POKER: In Stud games such as 7 Card Stud, the *lowest* card on board is *forced* to make a small bet on the first three cards (he cannot check or fold). In a $15/$30 Stud game for example, each player must ante $2, then the three-card starting hands are dealt. The lowest card on board, (usually a deuce) must "bring it in" for $5. This is designed to get the action started and is quite different from most "family-style" games in which the high card usually may bet or check on the first round. If another player wishes to raise, he must bring it up to $15 in accordance with the "$15/$30" mutuels for that game. From the fourth card on, however, the betting reverts to the high board acting first, with the option of betting or checking.

FLOP POKER: Since Hold'em and Omaha games begin with no cards on board, "blinds" are used rather than "antes." At $20/$40 Hold'em, for instance, the first two players to act must put in a "small blind" and "big blind" respectively. The amounts of the blinds are generally half the stakes. Thus, the first player must post $10 (small blind) and the second player puts up $20 (big blind) before any cards are dealt. In effect, the first player is forced to blindly bet $10 on his hand and the second player automatically raises it to $20.

Now, when the initial hole cards are dealt, it's up to the third player to either call the $20, raise to $40, or fold—then the action rotates around the table from there. If there are no raises when the action gets back to the small blind, since he already has $10 in, it's just $10 more for him to call. Likewise, the big blind, who has already paid $20, is in the hand automatically if nobody raised. If it had been raised to $40 while coming around, the small blind would then owe $30 and the big blind would owe $20, or fold.

The blinds, however, are *live*, since they posted their money "in the blind" as it were, and thus when the action gets back to them they may raise to $40 (or to $60 if it has already been raised). Thus, every player at the table will have had a chance to raise on the value of his hole cards.

Flop games bear one more key difference from Stud games. Since there are no individually owned board cards to determine who acts first, the small blind is first to act on every betting round (although he may bet or check after the first round). When that hand is over, the dealer will slide a small white puck (called the button) one seat clockwise. Now the player who was the small blind acts *last* on the entire *next* hand, while the big blind becomes the new small blind and all other players move up a notch. In that way, every player takes turns being the small blind, the big blind, third to act, and so on.

Section A

Universal Winning Poker Concepts

Chapter 1

Poker Is a Skill Game

The title to this chapter is a gross understatement. Make no mistake about it! There's a higher degree of skill involved in poker than any other casino game. At every poker table, there's a best player and a worst player. In fact, there's an old poker adage that says, "After playing your first few hands, take a look around the table and try to pick out the sucker. If you don't see any, it's you!" That's because a "ringer" in a weak game can be the "sucker" in a lineup of strong players—it's all relative.

But what is it that separates a good poker player from a bad one? There are many factors—but 77 of them will be presented in detail in the following pages. However, none can be more important than understanding Concept #1.

Concept #1: Playing Too Many Hands

Without question, the most common mistake losing poker players make is playing out too many of the hands they are dealt. You may be a cunning poker maven from the first bet to the river card, but if you don't pick your starting hands carefully, you'll be giving up more ground coming out of the gate than you can make up coming around the far turn. Why is this so? There are two very important reasons:

1. **Many hands are dealt, but only one hand can win the pot.**
2. **The best hand going in is more likely to be best coming out.**

So what does it mean? It means you must throw away all but your better starting hands—and the sooner, the better! To illustrate this principle, let me use 7 Card Stud as an example.

Before any cards are dealt, each of the eight players is a 7-to-1 underdog to win that next pot. But after the first three cards come out, all the odds get readjusted. Somebody, whoever it might be, is going to have the best starting hand, maybe a pair of Jacks. Somebody else is likely to have something like a pair of 7s with a King kicker. And another player might have a three-flush such as the 6/10/Q of clubs. The rest of the players will usually have less. Suddenly, instead of being a 7 to 1 shot, the three better hands all improve to 3-to-1 or 4-to-1 each. Everybody else becomes a longshot, some as high as 15-to-1!

If you have one of the weaker hands, it's silly to start matching the leaders dollar for dollar when they'll end up winning that particular pot much more often than you will. Just fold, and wait for a better hand with a better shot at the money.

A general rule of thumb is that you should be throwing away about 75 percent of all your starting hands without calling a bet. Many of the other 25 percent you'll fold at some point before the hand is over. Remember, second place pays the same as running dead last—nothing.

What it takes to constitute a playable starting hand depends not only upon the form of poker being played, but several factors unique to that particular hand. This will be addressed later in chapters on specific games.

Concept #2: The Best Hand Going In

In general, even though you have a good hand you should not enter a pot knowing that somebody has you beat going in. That's because of reason "2" in Concept #1. To fully appreciate its value, take a look at the two following starting hands from 7 Card Stud:

Hand 1　　　　　　　　**Hand 2**

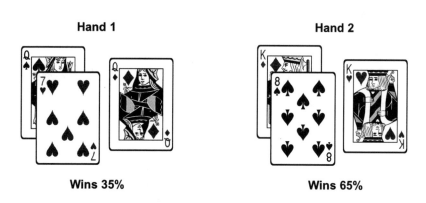

Wins 35%　　　　　　**Wins 65%**

The percentage figures beneath the hands tell you how often each hand will win the pot if both players duel heads-up to the end. The Kings are nearly a 2-to-1 favorite over the Queens. So if you come in raising with that pair of Queens, then the Kings re-raises you driving everybody else out, if you are convinced your opponent has the two Kings, it's not worth playing the hand out. Here's a cursory explanation of why.

In a $30/$60 Stud game, eight players ante $5 apiece and the low card brings it in for $10. Suppose you raise it to $30 with your two Queens and the Kings re-pops it to $60, setting the pot at $140 so far. If you call his $30 re-raise, then $30 more on 4th Street and another $60 on both 5th and on 6th Streets, there will be $470 in the pot by the time you get to the river. Thirty-five times out of 100, you'll pull in that $470 pot ($16,450 total), but you'll have paid an additional $180 all 100 times ($18,000). In reality, the betting gets more complicated than that due to the varied nuances that occur during the hand, but the fact holds that playing onward will cost you more money than you'll get back over time. (There will be more detailed strategy information on this subject in the 7 Stud chapter.)

Now here's a similar example from Texas Hold'em:

| **You Win 20%** | **Opponent #1 Wins 35%** | **Opponent #2 Wins 45%** |

Ace/Queen is normally a pretty good starting hand in Hold'em and usually worth a raise. But if you come in raising with it, then get raised and re-raised, you can be darn sure you don't have the best hand. You can't even feel comfortable if an Ace or a Queen flops, so you should just save those two extra bets and get out now.

These two examples were meant to illustrate that, ideally, you'd like to have the best hand coming in. Realistically, though, that's not always feasible, and there are indeed some hands that are worth playing even though it's apparent they're not best at the moment. Those are generally your "drawing hands."

A live three-flush such as the K/Q/8 of diamonds in 7 Stud, or a 10/J in Hold'em, when the flop is A-8-9 are two classic examples of drawing hands. Even though there might be a bet and a raise to you, if you make the flush in Stud, or the straight in Hold'em, you'll probably win a lot of money and should therefore play onward. But with hands that have their own initial starting strength (such as pairs in Stud, or high cards in Hold'em), the general principle to remember is that *you usually shouldn't play a starting hand that is likely to be chasing a better hand of the same type!*

Concept #3: Poker is a Game of Mistakes

It's a well known fact that both blackjack and live poker are two "beatable" casino games. Winning strategy at casino blackjack is quite an exact science. When you have 14 against a 5 up in blackjack, you should definitely stand. You know proof positive that the dealer will take a card, even if she turns up a 10 in the hole and already has you beaten with 15. Also, most blackjack bets are for even money. With these constants known, determining the correct play is nothing more than a lengthy mathematical problem. Once that's worked out though, blackjack's proper strategy is gospel.

Poker is much more complicated than that. In poker, you often don't know how your opponent will play his hand. It's the equivalent of your blackjack dealer turning up that 15, looking around the board and saying, "Hmm, should I take a hit here or should I stand?"

That's how your opponent's free will in poker creates a whole new set of problems for you. When you bet into him, sometimes he'll fold, sometimes he'll call, and sometimes he'll raise. And when he does raise, he'll occasionally be bluffing. Besides that, each player has his own standards for when he'll do each. Combine that with the ever-changing odds on your money (the varying sizes of the pots) and correct poker strategy becomes a very *inexact* science. In fact, it's actually more of an *art*.

It's fine to understand that, mathematically, you shouldn't call a pair of Aces with a pair of Kings. But how do you know your opponent has that pair of Aces? Sometimes your opponent may play his hand as though he has Aces when he actually has a four-flush. That's where the art comes in.

You see, poker starts out as an "odds game" and ends up as a "mind game," while all other casino games are strictly odds games. In the end, winning play in poker boils down to a combination of reading your opponent's hand, guessing how he'll play it, and evaluating your chances of beating him either through deception or by making the best hand. Handling all these variables perfectly is virtually impossible.

A blackjack pro executes his plays according to a complex but completely "canned" procedure and he must play virtually mistake-free to win. But poker is, in fact, *a game of mistakes*. Everybody makes them. The good news is that the players err against each other. When you make a mistake in a hand, your opponent gains an edge. Later on, if he makes a mistake against you, you gain an edge back. In the end, *the player who makes the fewest mistakes wins the most money*.

This is an important concept to recognize; nobody plays perfect poker. First, you need a fundamental knowledge of what hands are worth playing against what other hands. Then you want to determine which hand you're up against so you can apply that fundamental knowledge. The best way to develop your "reading" abilities is to pay attention when you're out of the hands. Focus on one player and try to figure out what he's holding. Learn which players have what tendencies. You'll find this task easier when you're not absorbed in playing your own cards.

Does Bulldozer Bob like to raise on a four-flush? Will Loose Larry stand a bet and a raise with just a mediocre hand? Does Tight Tommy ever bluff? These things will tell you how to play each of them later on when you're in a hand together. A perceptive read can make it correct to raise Loose

Larry with the same hand that you should fold against Tight Tommy. And if you blow a read here and there, shake it off. Remember, you just have to make fewer mistakes than the next guy!

Concept #4: The Money Usually Goes to the Aggressor

There's another common mistake many losing poker players make; it's not quite as foolish as Concept #1, but it is still plenty costly. That's picking out a good starting hand and then playing it *passively*. Doing that is just asking to get beaten.

To do things right, first you want to throw away all your weak starting hands. Then you want to immediately take command of the pot with your good ones. This is the basic "one-two" combination of winning poker play. Fundamentally, your goal is to either win the pot any way you can, or be out of it.

Often when an inexperienced player is dealt a good starting hand, he's afraid of running off his customers. He thinks he should slowplay it for a bet or two, then lower the boom. This is all wrong! Winning poker is more a game of knocking people out than sucking people in. Why?

As the pot gradually builds, opponents with inferior hands accumulate the opportunity to win much more money than it will cost to call. A $100 pot may cost only a $20 bet to call on the flop in Hold'em or on 4th Street in 7 Stud. Later on in the hand, the price can become even more attractive. You want to shut your opponents out before this pot becomes a good value. Don't worry about losing everybody with your buried Aces. Usually at least one player will find something to chase you down with—and that's just about perfect.

Even if you do win a small pot right now, that's fine. Realize that if the hand got played all the way out, and you subtracted all your wins from the times you got run down, your net average gain might be less than the size of that small pot. Winning an anemic pot early is far from a tragedy. In the vast majority of cases, when it looks like you've started out with the best hand, your credo should be *either pay up or get out of my pot*!

Concept #5: You Need a Better Hand to Call Than to Bet Yourself

It may sound like double talk at first, but Concept #5 makes perfect sense once you think about it. Let's embellish this important principle by illustrating a poker scenario I'm sure you're familiar with.

You're playing 5 Card Draw, Jacks or better to open. Sitting in the last seat, you're dealt a pair of Jacks—minimum openers. One by one, the players check, so you anticipate opening as the action comes around towards you. But then the player just in front of you opens. What's your correct play? Answer: You should fold. Why is that, when you had a good enough hand to open yourself? It's really quite simple.

While player after player was checking in the example above, that probably meant nobody had a good enough hand to open. If the pot is still unopened by the time the action gets to you, your Jacks may very well be the best hand—pure and simple. So go ahead and bet. But if it gets opened before you, that player has to have a pair of Jacks—or better! Now you're almost certainly chasing. And remember, the best hand going in is more likely to be the best coming out. So, where it would have been right to bet a pair of Jacks before, now they're not even worth a call.

We used the most basic poker form in the world to illustrate this point, but it holds true in every kind of poker.

What you do is act upon the *latest* information you have and then bet, raise or fold accordingly.

Here's an example from a typical hand of $30/$60 at 7 Card Stud as it's played in the casino. On your first three cards you have:

A deuce is forced in for $10 and the first three players fold. You're thinking of either calling the $10 or raising it to $30 when it gets to you. But then a player with a 10 up raises it to $30 and another player showing a 9 calls the raise. All of a sudden, the deuce isn't your concern. What did the 10 raise with and why did the 9 call that raise? This new information tells you that your hand is probably second or third best! So give it up!

Here's another example, this one from Texas Hold'em. The initial hole cards are dealt and one player calls the blinds before it gets to you. Your hand is:

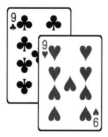

So you raise, driving out everybody behind you, but the original caller pays off your raise. The flop comes down:

If your opponent just checks, there's a pretty good chance he missed the flop, making your hand best at the moment—so you should probably bet. He may very well fold and give you the pot. But if your opponent bets he quite possibly has Kings—or at least Queens, since those are just the kinds of cards he might have limped in with up front. Now you probably shouldn't even call! There again is a practical example of how it's right to bet your hand if nobody else has yet bet, but you should fold if there's already been a bet.

Concept #6: Many Hands Are a "Raise or Fold" Situation

Every time there's a bet made to you in a hand of poker you have three choices; call, raise, or fold. Nearly all winning players do a lot of folding and a good amount of raising, but not very much calling. Take a look at the illustration on the following page.

The game is $30/$60 Seven Card Stud. Eight players have anted $5 each. The low card was forced in for $10 with a deuce up. One by one, the other players have folded and the bet finally gets around to you. Looking down, you have a split pair of 3s with a 7 kicker. The last player between you and the deuce has a Queen up. What should you do?

If you say fold, I have no particular quarrel with you. If you say raise, I readily agree. But if you say call, I've got a problem with that. Why? Because if you call, three events can happen:

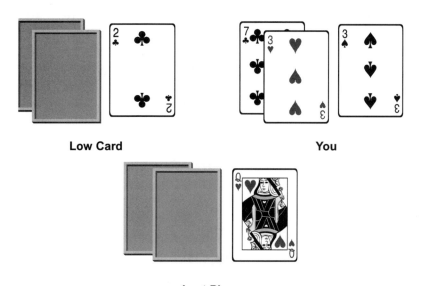

Low Card   **You**

Last Player

Event #1: The Queen can raise, making you wish you had folded.

Event #2: The Queen can call, putting you in a three-way pot with a fairly weak hand.

Event #3: The Queen can fold, leaving just you and the deuce in the pot.

If event #1 happens, you'll be glad you didn't do the raising, and should probably now fold. But if either #2 or #3 happens, there's a good chance you'd have won the pot right there had you raised.

The extra money you'd have wasted by raising in event #1 is $20 (the difference between just calling $10 and raising it to $30). But the pot you might have won in both other events is $50! If you fear the Queen, perhaps because he's a very aggressive player, or you think he can just plain outplay you, then it might be best to stay out of this hand. But if you're going to play, you can't get rid of the deuce unless you raise—and just calling is inviting the overcard Queen in as well. No. Figure out if you feel strong enough to do battle with this hand and either raise or fold.

This was just one isolated example of a "raise or fold" situation—but every form of poker is littered with them. These two elements, playing combined with raising, work so well together that whenever you have a hand you feel is worth playing, you should consider raising! If you don't think you can profitably raise, then there's a fair chance you shouldn't even be calling. Read this next statement and remember it well: *In poker, a chronic caller is a chronic loser!*

Concept #7: The Courage to Fold

Having the discipline to wait for a good starting hand before getting involved in a pot is one thing. But there's another, equally important decision that repeatedly requires not only discipline, but courage as well. It often arises after you've folded several consecutive starts and finally get a real nice hand to play—then something goes wrong.

At the first instant when this happens, your initial reaction might be denial. You think to yourself, "Hey, I folded a ton of junk hands and now I've got this nice premium start— I'm not giving it up!" As I said, this is a decision that takes courage—the courage to face up to the fact that your good hand is probably no good—and you must abandon it.

Situations like this arise in every poker form. Following is a basic example from each of the four games covered in this book.

7 CARD STUD: You've folded starting hand after starting hand for what seems like forever and are finally dealt:

You raise and are called by a couple of players, one of them showing a 10 up. Now, on 4th Street, he pairs that door-card 10 on board and bets the top bet. If he's anything other than a reckless player, and you've seen no other 10s, it's time to fold (see Concept #33 for a more detailed analysis). The pot is still small and it's just too likely that he called your initial raise with a split pair of 10s, now giving him trips—and there may be four big bets to call. Even if he started out with a small buried pair or a three-flush, you are not in an enviable position. All things considered, you're anywhere from a modest favorite to a huge underdog. Save the money for your next good hand.

TEXAS HOLD'EM: You're dealt two pretty Queens in the pocket and raise before the flop. Two players, who limped in before you, call your raise and the flop comes down:

The first player bets and the second player calls. Your two Queens are worthless—dump them. Yes, it's possible the first player may have bet the flop just to see if anybody else could call with that scary Ace on board. But when the second player calls, one of them has an Ace almost for sure. You're going to end up eating those two Queens.

OMAHA HI/LO 8 or Better: You're dealt a dream hand of A-A-2-3 with both Aces suited. Five players stay in to see the flop. Here it comes:

Unfortunately, you don't have any clubs. There's a bet, a call and then a raise. With an 8 low no longer being possible, you've got a good hand gone bad—fold it. Yes, you've got Aces and Queens. But somebody quite likely already has three Queens or a full house, and, if not, a club flush will develop another third of the time (not to mention that any 8, 9, 10, or K will make a straight likely). You probably need an Ace specifically to win, giving you just two "outs" (the other two Aces). And two-outers are known as sucker calls in poker.

7 STUD HI/LO 8 or Better: After folding a dozen consecutive hands you're finally dealt:

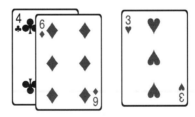

to start out with and raise coming in. Your fourth card is another 6 giving you a small pair and a smooth three-card low with some remote straight potential. On 5th Street you pick up a low draw with an 8 while your two opponents now show:

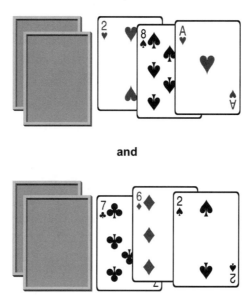

and

The Ace high bets and you're next. Fold—they've out-drawn you. If you call, you may very well get raised by the 7/6/2 and maybe even re-raised by the Ace. All this while you are still struggling to make some sort of a hand—a way too costly endeavor.

These are just a few of the countless scenarios that will test your poker character every time you play. The lesson here is that even though you enter the pot with good starting hands, many of them will go bad before it's over. Sometimes it will be subtle and sometimes it will be glaring, but it will always be disappointing. If you can't muster the courage to reverse direction and release your hand in these spots, you'll probably still end up as a losing poker player!

Chapter 2

Luck and Streaks in Poker

Poker, like any form of gambling, is loaded with volatility that affects all players, be they strong or weak. A poor poker player will occasionally have some huge wins—often bigger than a pro will have because a poor player will expose himself to many gambling risks that a pro won't take. When he gets lucky in those spots, he destroys everybody—maybe all night long. A lucky run of cards can do miracles for you. Unfortunately, things can also go the other way. There will be periods during which even an excellent player simply cannot buy a win, and a bad player just doesn't lose.

The purpose of this chapter is to help you understand what luck and streaks can do *for* you, and what they can do *to* you. The second effect is the more important of the two. Believe it or not, when you're running good there generally isn't a whole lot you can do to make things better. But when you're going bad, and you will go bad, you have to be very careful and very well tuned in. That brings us to our first working concept on luck and streaks in poker.

Concept #8: Bankroll Requirements

To be a long-term winner at poker your pockets must be deep enough to survive the eventual droughts that you'll experience along the way. Much has been written about bankrolling a winning gambling endeavor. Many essays on the subject go into technical calculations of standard deviation, gambler's ruin formula, etc., and most of them are accurate. But all you really want to know is the answer to this question: "How much money do I need to be able to ride out my negative swings if I'm basically a winner at the game?"

Here's an adequate nutshell answer to that question. A total bankroll of 500 "big bets" should see you through a year's worth of poker peaks and valleys, if you're at least a break-even player who plays a couple of nights a week. A big bet is $30 in a $15/$30 game and $100 at $50/$100 stakes. The totals may seem like a lot, but you can occasionally go through 500 hours worth of cards that just won't give you an even break. That will cost you a lot of money. Therefore, if you're a regular $30/$60 player, you should have about $30K that you can get to if you should need it. If you don't have it, somewhere, some day you may very well find yourself betting your case money—and that's no way to live. If you haven't got the 500 bets, drop down to smaller limits where you do.

Now, suppose you're making an out-of-town trip to casino country for four or five days of poker action. While there, you'll probably spend 30 or 40 hours at the tables. How many "bullets" should you bring with you? About 150 big bets will get you through all but the very worst runs of cards. That means if you'll be playing in a mixture of $20/$40, $30/$60 and $40/$80 games the whole time, you'll want a trip stake of about $9,000 (150 x $60) to keep you in ammo.

Finally, what about a single night of poker? How much is enough? I've found that 60 big bets will cover me on all but those rare nights from hell. That means if you're heading out for a night of $30/$60 action, then something like $3,500 will keep you armed well enough to play right. Even though you may hardly ever lose the $3,500, there will be times you'll be stuck that much and will end up the night losing, say, $2,000. You don't want to cut off your "comeback" opportunities if you're a winning player. To summarize, here is a concise list of bankroll requirements for a break-even or winning poker player.

Length of Time	Bankroll Needed
one session	60 big bets
five-day trip	150 big bets
a year (500–1000 hours)	500 big bets

Now, I've heard some players say if you can't win on 25 or 30 big bets, it's not going to be your night and you're better off packing it in. Well, that's another thing that you, and they, need to understand about luck, which is:

Concept #9: Luck Has No Will and No Plan

Being unable to win once you get stuck 30 bets is primarily a psychological limitation. Poker has such an integral psychological connection to the other players that if you decide you can't win—you can't! When you allow yourself to feel whipped and downtrodden, you begin playing submissively, and poker is no game for submissive players. When you're losing, the cards and the chips don't know you're stuck. It's true that the other players do, but that's not an edge for them unless you turn it into one. If you're fully aware that your losing was just a combination of bad cards/bad beats and you're still on your game, your right move is to *suck it up and tough it out.*

WIPING THE SLATE CLEAN: Some players hate losing so much that they just can't play well from behind. They'd rather call it a day and come back tomorrow. That's their own personal shortcoming. When they sit down at the table the next day, in their minds they may be starting out even, but check the record book and their bankrolls, because in reality, they're still stuck the 30 bets from yesterday! Like I said, it's a self-imposed psychological barrier.

If your head is on straight, then your chance to start making some money is just as good right now as it will be tomorrow (maybe even better if your opponents are playing you as though you can't catch a card). You must train yourself to think this way and you'll see that it's true. And once you realize it's true, you'll welcome the opportunity to turn your 30 bet loser into a 15 or 20 bet loser which should become your revised goal on this particular day. Remember: *money regained is the same as money won!*

I disagree with the general view that your opponents play better against you when you're losing. That's only true if losing has knocked you off your game. When you can't make a hand, your opponents tend to play you as though you're an empty seat. They tend to play right through you. But let me ask you this question: Is that how you should play a good player who's still on his game and, in reality, is just as likely to make a hand as you, even though it's been a while since he's done so? Who would be playing good and who would be playing bad in that scenario? Once you've gotten behind in a game, your chances for the rest of the session are largely up to you. Nobody fears you. Nobody gives you any respect. If you can stay focused, this is *their* mistake and you should be able to exploit it.

Part of being a winning player is the ability to handle adversity—and adjust to it. You can still make money when you're stuck, but you may have to make it a little different way. You won't be able to steal a pot, because nobody will believe you since you haven't been able to show anyone a hand. You will, however, get paid off in spots where you wouldn't if you'd been running over the game. The very next pot you win may well contain a few extra bets because you didn't get the respect you deserved. That's because poker players, like most gamblers, mistakenly believe that streaks are more likely to continue than stop—good streaks and bad streaks alike. Which brings us to the next concept.

Concept #10: How Real Are "Rushes" in Poker?

"He really knows how to play a rush!" How often have you heard that said about somebody who has just made a huge win in a poker game? The player in question got on a roll and just kept pushing it. And what happened? He made hand after hand after hand, even with mediocre starts. What about this phenomenon? Is there any truth to the theory that when you're hot you're likely to stay hot? Should you open it up when you're running good to maximize your win? This is an important question, so keep your mind open and read this true story.

I was playing $50/$100 Hold'em a while back. I entered the pot raising from the #4 seat with pocket Kings and found myself heads up with George on the button. The flop came down:

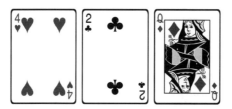

I bet; George called. The turn card was an 8. I led out with a bet and got called again. Then an offsuit 7 came on the river making the final board 2/4/Q/8/7. I bet right out and

George raised! Now George was an action player who could have had A/Q as easily as 5/6 or 4/4. I called and wouldn't have been surprised to see any of the three. But no! To my confusion, he turned over:

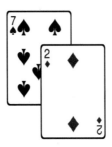

George's 7s and deuces beat my two Kings fair and square.

Now, it's a commonly held opinion that of the 169 starting hands you can be dealt in Texas Hold'em, an unsuited 7/deuce ranks dead last. That's because they're the two lowest cards that can't reach to a straight. Good old George had taken the worst Hold'em hand in the deck and ran down pocket Kings like they were chopped liver. While stacking his chips, he explained that the only reason he called to see the flop was because *he was on a rush!* The cards were coming his way, so he figured he'd play the heat. Was George doing the right thing here? Most gamblers would say yes. But then again, most gamblers are losers. Mathematics and scientific experiments generally say *no!*

I regularly practice both poker and blackjack at home. Now, a typical blackjack player will jack up his bets after winning a couple in a row to capitalize on his streaks. I see this practice done so regularly in the casino that I decided to track all my blackjack streaks of three wins in a row while practicing at home. I wanted to see how I would do on all those "4th" hands immediately following three straight wins. If betting your streaks has any merit to it, then I should make money on all those 4th hands combined. It took roughly 2,400 hands with a six-deck shoe to amass 100 separate streaks of at least three wins in a row.

So how did I do on all the 4th hands of those 100 streaks? I won 45, lost 50, and pushed 5. My "rush" had ended on the very next hand more often than it continued! Now consider this. The *random* probabilities for a hand of blackjack are that you'll will win 43, lose 48, and push 9 out of 100. Hold onto that thought for a moment.

Another well-known gaming writer, John Grochowski of the *Chicago Sun-Times,* recently went around to the local craps tables and charted 1,000 occasions on which the dice made two straight passes—just to see what would happen on all those third pass attempts. Now, the random probabilities on the pass line at craps are that there will be 493 passes and 507 misses out of 1,000 attempts. In John's experiment, the actual outcomes for all the third pass attempts immediately following two passes in a row went—489 passes and 511 misses. Limited sample size that each of these experiments were, it appeared we both had just about the same chance to win that next bet right after two or three wins in a row as *at any other time!*

I wasn't surprised by these results. I'm a firm believer in the postulate that when gambling with inanimate objects, every next bet is a brand new ball game. You see, the roulette wheels, the dice and the cards are mindless. They just don't care whether "red" has come up 14 times in a row at roulette or two passes have been made in craps or three decisions in a row have gone the blackjack player's way. I think you'll find that in all such cases all over the world combined, "red" will come up just as often on the 15th spin as at any other time, the third pass will come up just as often as the first pass, and the fourth hand will be won just as many times as blackjack math dictates.

However, when it comes to poker, things might be, and probably are *different.* Why would that be? Let's go back to the Hold'em hand at the beginning of this story. I'm convinced George wasn't any more likely to make a second pair at the river merely because he had been hot. But he, just like many other players at that same table, believed differently. So a believer *plays more hands* when he's running good. He raises more aggressively with a draw, anticipating that he'll fill. He enters the pot with substandard hands expecting to improve them.

If he were playing against robots as in craps or black-jack, this would usually be suicide. Ahh, but the poker player is not playing against robots. He's playing against human gamblers who believe in the same things he does. So what happens? They fear him. They believe he's temporarily blessed and tend to back out of his way. When he raises, they fold more often than they should because he's "on a rush." They may tend to check with the better hand, allowing the "hot man" to draw free cards. When he bluffs, they're more inclined to believe him. Thus, *it all becomes a self-fulfilling prophesy.*

It's similar to frightened investors expecting the bottom to fall out of the stock market, so they sell off in fear. And what happens? The bottom falls out due to a major sell-off. Because of the interactive human element, a poker rush can be perpetuated simply through belief. However, *without the unwitting help of the other players, many rushes would die young.*

Think about this. What if you had just won three pots in a row, but you were the only person at the table who believed in rushes? If you lowered your starting requirements and began playing substandard hands, would that be good play or bad play? When you force those substandard hands aggressively against your non-believing opponents who are playing you hand by hand, are you gaining command of the table, or blowing off chips? And when you improve just as often as you're supposed to by finishing third with the third best starting hand are you playing a rush, or going on tilt? Amongst a table full of nonbelievers, a person who thinks he's on a rush can suddenly become the sucker by virtue of his own reckless play.

Successfully pushing a rush usually tends to work better in lower stakes games than at the upper limits. The $5/$10 players are more likely to believe in the "short-term destiny" of the cards. Higher limit players are less likely to be intimidated by somebody who just followed up a full house with a "three-outer" on the next hand to win a second big pot. With all that said, I have two pieces of advice concerning rushes:

1. If you observe a player trying to "push a rush," he'll likely be forcing the action with cards that don't warrant it. Watch him and look for a solid hand to get in there with. Then step submissively in his path and let him try to run over you. You'll put a sudden end to a few players' rushes that way.

2. If you've just won a few consecutive pots and feel compelled to "play the rush," look around the table to see if the field appears intimidated by your current "hot run." If by and large, they appear unshaken, you've lost your valuable accomplices—so you better behave yourself!

Concept #11: The Right Time to Quit

They are age-old questions. When have you made enough money to lock up your winnings for the day? And how do you know when it's time to cut your losses and throw in the towel? These questions are generally looked at so illogically by players who are otherwise perceptive and logical in most other areas of their game. Yet the answer is so simple, because *determining if it's time to quit has nothing to do with whether you are winning or losing.*

Sound like nonsense? Well, just put your old beliefs aside for a moment and answer these next two questions as logically as you can.

First, suppose you sat down at a casino poker table with a crew of total strangers. After half an hour you realized you were playing with a table full of world class professionals. You were by far the weakest player, but had made a few key hands and were currently winning. You even bluffed one of them out of a pot. What should you do? Simple answer. The fact is, you're hopelessly outclassed. Since you'll almost certainly be beaten senseless if you continue to buck heads with them, you should definitely get up and quit right now. Ahh, but what if you were already losing? Same answer; get away from there ASAP before they gut you!

Okay, now let's reverse it and say you've discovered you're playing with a bunch of complete suckers. You are head and shoulders above them all, but you've taken a couple of tough beats and are getting slaughtered. What's your move?

Since you outclass the field, the "cream" will eventually rise to the top if you stick with it. Therefore you should stay put even though you're stuck. And what if you were already winning? You're likely to keep right on winning, so again, stay put.

Well then, can you see that whether you should quit or keep gambling has nothing to do with winning or losing? Assuming you've got the time, the money and all your senses about you, there are only two determinants:

1. **If you've got the edge, you should always keep playing.**
2. **If you're an underdog you should never have started, so quit right now.**

Forget everything else. It's impossible to accurately guess how the cards will run during the next hour, or even the next hand. Your best estimate of what to do is always based upon your odds to win from this moment going forward. If you're "stuck like a pig" and getting even seems hopeless, then forget about getting even! Your only question should be, "If I stay in the game, am I likely to win something starting right now?" If you're still playing well and the game conditions remain good, your chance to pick up a few bucks starting now are just as good as if you come back tomorrow or next week.

On the other hand if you've been psychologically handicapped by the beats you've taken and can't shake it off, then you have no edge and better pack it in. Just understand that you will have lost your edge as a result of your own doing, and that's a perspective you need to work on.

As for predicting the future, there is no "curve" to look at when you're winning that will tell you when it's over. There is no "support level" at the bottom that will predict a poker free-fall. That stuff is all in your head. Whether you stick around or go home and come back a month later, to the cards and the chips, that'll just be your next hand. And all your hands will piggyback end to end as if it were one long session anyway.

Concept #12: You Can't Beat Poker By Quitting When You're Ahead

What do you suppose your chances are of beating an honest coin flip game? It's a balanced coin and you're getting even money on every bet. The answer is that you're a 50/50 shot, of course. But did you know there's a way to book a winner on roughly 80 percent of your playing sessions in this game if you manage your money right? How? Simply by quitting every time you get one flip ahead. The only losers you'll book are when you lose your first flip and never get ahead, even for a moment.

Sound like a winning strategy? Unfortunately, it's not. There's still one problem you can't get away from. No matter what, you're going to end up winning 50 percent of all your flips. And at even money per flip, where does that put you? Dead even, doesn't it? "Well, how can this be if I win most of my sessions?" you ask. Let me show you with a similar poker illustration.

Suppose you've been a dead break even poker player over the last five years. So to gain a little extra edge you decide you're going to quit every time you get ahead, even if it's after the very first hand. Now let's say that on two separate days you won the first hand you were dealt and were up $300 each time. True to your game plan, you locked up the $300 both times and high-tailed it home. For those two sessions, your poker log would look like this:

Win	**+$300**
Win	**+$300**
TOTAL	**+$600**

That's two neat little wins, no losses and a $600 gain. By quitting winners you've averted the possibility of a loss and can start out fresh next time—with another 50/50 shot. The only problem is, you've also averted the equal possibility of a larger win. You see, as a break-even player you'd have been as likely to win a few more dollars as lose back that same amount had you kept on playing. In fact if you played onward both times, winning an extra $500 once and losing back $500 the other time would be perfectly normal and average for you, wouldn't it? Then your poker log would look like this:

Win	**+$800**
Lose	**-$200**
TOTAL	**+$600**

Now you'd have one win and one loss, but the same $600 net gain. Stop right here and think hard about that. The only thing quitting winners accomplished was averting further swings in both directions. So quitting as soon as you got ahead improved your won/lost record, but not your bottom line because *you can't improve your chances of winning overall just by stopping and starting at selective points.*

When you come back to play next time, there will be no difference between that last hand you didn't take because you quit and the first hand of your next playing session.

Remember, they're both just the next hand. The only place there was any effective break was in your mind. Gambling is all one long game even if we don't think of it that way. You're eventually going to end up right where your poker compass is pointed, whether you take one long trip or many short ones.

In our minds, we tend to measure our progress by the day. But our pocketbooks can't feel where one day ended and the next began. When you quit just to lock up a guaranteed winner, you're merely stopping to admire your progress at a favorable interval, but you're not altering that progress. You might as well sit at the table and say to yourself, "Okay, I'm $300 ahead, I quit." Then get out a notebook pad, log down your $300 winner—and take the next hand; it's the same as leaving and coming back tomorrow.

Struggling players do it all the time. If they slip to just a few dollars ahead, they quit to preserve the winner because winners don't come that easily. If they're losing, they keep pressing and pressing until they either climb a little in front, or get hopelessly stuck and finally give up. This limits the size of many of their wins, but not their losses. All they've done is trade an equal number of similar sized wins and losses for lots of small winners and a few ugly beatings.

When we play poker, we're on one continuous journey landscaped with endless hills and valleys. Each of us is headed towards our own individual destination determined only by the quality of our play. We can almost always park on a hill rather than in a valley, but the road is still going to the same place!

Understand that if you're a losing player, you're more likely to lose than win whether it's right now or tomorrow. There's simply no other day on the calendar where you can hide from that. The only way to become a sustained winner at poker is to outplay your opponents. Trying to time your luck just won't work. And the more you focus on irrelevant game tactics such as these, the less attention you'll devote toward figuring out how to play winning poker. Then you'll be just another frustrated loser, and you won't even understand why.

Chapter 3

The Poker Sense of Betting

In playing your poker hands you'll have endless opportunities to bet, raise, call and fold. Sometimes your play will be automatic, but most times it won't. If you flop trips in Omaha, for example, and somebody bets into you, it may be right to raise, but it may also be better to just call or sometimes even to fold.

When your best move is to fold, your problems are over for that hand. But when you belong in the hand, there are a number of ways to proceed with it, and some ways are better than others. That's where betting with poker sense comes in handy. The concepts in this chapter will attempt to illustrate the logic, or "poker sense" behind checking, betting, calling, raising and check/raising. By understanding them you'll find ways to "outplay" your opponents when the opportunities present themselves, which is what winning poker is all about.

Concept #13: The Importance of Betting

The majority of times when you have a playable hand you should be betting. The thing that makes betting most important is if there are still more cards to come, which is most of the time. That's because your bet may drive players out who might end up beating you if they could play for free.

Have you ever played in a friendly family quarter-and-half poker game? Remember when they played 5 Card Stud and the high upcard would act first on the initial deal? If that high card was, let's say, a Jack, there's a pretty fair chance he'd just check—because after all, this is a friendly family game. And what would happen? It would often go, check, check, check all the way around the table.

Well, somebody had to be making a tactical mistake. If that Jack had any decent card in the hole, he needed to bet that quarter to either pressure weaker hands into folding or making a bad call. Giving them a free ride is just giving up his edge.

Now later on in that same hand, maybe another player makes an open pair of 8s and bets only 25¢ rather than the half dollar limit. Again, this player would be giving his opponents a cheap shot at outdrawing him. He may think he's reeling the suckers in, but what he's really doing is just asking to get beat. The critical principle to understand is that *once the pot starts to build, you would rather your opponents fold than call.*

That's generally the more profitable overall scenario. Unless your hand is just plain huge, your proper play is to bet the limit to discourage opponents from calling and improving. If they want to pay the price, then fine; either you've taxed them to chase you or they've given you the pot. At upper limit casino poker, you can be assured you won't find many players giving you free or cheap cards when they have a good hand. So realize that whenever you're in the lead, you're vulnerable and you want the opposition out of your pot!

Concept #14: When NOT to Bet

Although it's true that you should generally bet with a good hand, there are nevertheless some situations in which you should check, even with the probable winner. When would that be? Take a look at the following 7 Card Stud scenario:

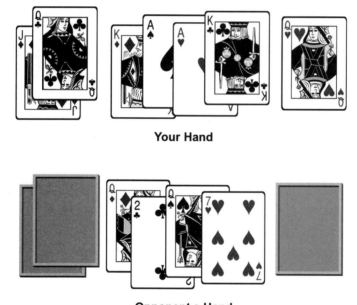

Your Hand

Opponent s Hand

All seven cards have been dealt and you have just one remaining opponent. You started the hand with J/Q/K and proceeded to make Aces and Kings on board. Since you're high, it's up to you to bet or check. What's your correct play?

Look at all the cards carefully. If your opponent has just a pair of Queens or even Queens up, you have him beaten. He can't possibly have trip Queens since you hold the other two Queens in your hand. It's also impossible for him to have a straight or a flush due to his four different suits on board and the wide gaps between each card. About the only way you can lose this hand is to something like deuces full or maybe 7s full. You're an odds on favorite to have the best hand, yet betting in this spot would be fundamentally wrong. Why? Because the entire strength of your hand is exposed with no more cards coming. Thus, your opponent will fold unless he has you beat. That's the key! As a result, you'd be making a bet you can lose but cannot win.

With all the cards already out, a bet on your part can no longer help you win the pot by stopping your opponent from improving his hand. The winning hand, whichever it is, has already been dealt.

Think about it. If you bet, your opponent is not going to fold if he's got a full house. Also, he won't pay you off if he has Queens up since he's already looking at Aces up. So you can't buy the pot if your Aces up are a loser and you can't make any more money with them if they're a winner.

If you bet in this spot, most of the time your opponent will just fold and you'll rake in a pot that would have been yours even if you had checked. But the problem is, your pot will not contain his last call. In fact, there's virtually no way for you to win that last bet. However, that one odd time when he does have a full house, you'll lose a pot you were going to lose anyway, plus that last bet which you never could have won (and maybe a raise besides)! This is usually the condition you're facing whenever what you show is all you have. For that reason when all the cards are out and you're high on board with the full strength of your hand exposed, you should just check.

Checking is the correct play because if you bet, you'll either win the pot without gaining that last bet, or lose the pot along with your last bet. You have nothing to gain by betting, but you do have something to lose—*that last bet on the end*!

If you do check and your opponent bets into you, that opens up a whole other strategic topic. But if he's bluffing and you call, then you have succeeded in winning an extra bet on the end—and you got it by checking.

Concept #15: Raising and Winning Go Hand in Hand

There are many different styles of poker players. You have "calling stations," "maniacs," "tight rocks," "empty seats," and more. Among them all, there's one style of player who almost never wins, and that's the "calling station." A calling station will usually call your raise when you've got a good hand, but will seldom make a raise when he has one. Doing this, he allows you to increase the stakes when *you're* loaded, but keeps them small when *he's* got the stuff. It should seem obvious that this is counterproductive.

Most winning players, on the other hand, are somewhat tight and somewhat aggressive. They don't call many raises, but they make a good share of their own. Why is controlled raising a winning tactic? There are a few reasons.

First, if you come into a hand calling, you've merely bought yourself the right to improve your hand which might win in a showdown. But if you come in raising, there's the chance you might win the pot right now without ever seeing a showdown. Or you might catch a scary card right after you raise which allows you to "bet and take it" on the next round. So calling gives you one way to win while raising gives you a number of ways.

Next, when you raise it tends to put your opponents back on their heels a bit. They're more inclined to check to you on the next card than if you hadn't raised. As a result, you often get to dictate the pace of the hand. If the cards fall such that you want a free ride on the next round, you frequently can get it. If you want to keep on betting, you can have it that way, too.

The main reason, however, that raising (with a good hand) is a winning tactic is that it tends to turn your opponent's calls from profitable to unprofitable because your raise cuts down their "pot odds" (see Concept #22). Many of your opponents who hold inferior hands will realize this when you raise and get out. Some others will just make a bad call and although they'll sometimes beat you, on average their calling will contribute to your stack. That's why *if you are not folding, you should usually be betting or raising.*

Concept #16: However, Sometimes You Should Just Call

If you always had your way in poker, you'd have the best hand going every time and you'd be constantly betting and raising. In fact if you can't bet or raise, you might want to question whether you should be in the hand at all.

But sometimes you clearly belong in the hand, yet you should only call. These times occur routinely when you're on a draw for a straight or a flush. Still, there are other occasions when you know you're beaten at the moment, but your hand is nevertheless worth a play. Here's one of those times. The game is 7 Card Stud:

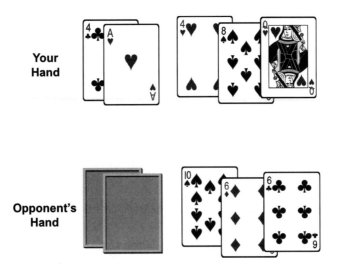

Whether your opponent has 10s up or just a pair of 6s, you're trailing. If he didn't play his hand as though he started with two 10s; or even if he did and your Ace and Queen are live, you're a close enough underdog that folding would be wrong. And since raising would be unlikely to accomplish anything, the proper play is to just call. Here's another calling situation, this one from Texas Hold'em. You have:

and on the turn the board is:

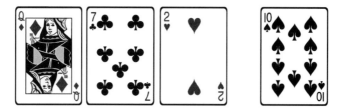

The aggressor appears to have been betting a pair of Queens all the way. Besides your two overcards (the Ace and King) you can now make the nut straight with an inside Jack. That gives you ten likely "outs" (three Aces, three Kings and four Jacks) rather than just six and an easy call. Even if your opponent has, say, K/Q you've made a proper call having only seven outs.

Calling situations come up again and again in poker, but they usually occur later in the hand once substantial money is already in the pot. At that point, you know you're chasing but the pot odds make it worthwhile.

Concept #17: Check/Raising—A Potent Offensive Weapon

Let's say you're playing $20/$40 Texas Hold'em and you've got pocket Aces. So you raise it up and everybody folds except the big blind. The flop is an innocuous looking:

The big blind checks, you bet $20 and again are called. The turn card is the 7 of hearts, putting a flush draw and a possible straight draw on the board. Once more, the big blind checks. Feeling safe as long as no flush card or straight card comes, you bet $40 virtually hoping for another call. Then it comes—the ominous check/raise!

This is one of the most unsettling developments in the game of poker, being check/raised late in the hand. What could he have raised you with? Did he trap you on the flop with three 8s? Has he merely got a Queen with a good kicker and thinks he has you beat? Perhaps you even have him trapped with two Kings in the hole—or he might have something like the King/Queen of hearts giving him top pair with a flush draw. Since he has no way of knowing your hand is as strong as it is, you call, suddenly fearing that you may be the hunted rather than the hunter.

The finish comes swiftly. The last card is an offsuit 3, no straight, no flush. The big blind bets out, you call and he shows you pocket 8s for a set of trips. As you can see, the check/raise is a deadly tool that can gain a player extra bets with his winning hands. This was just one example.

Check/Raising for Value

When check/raising as a trap play, you generally want to wait until you feel your opponent is committed to playing the hand all the way through. The most common point for a value check/raise is just before the last card (as in the preceding Hold'em example). By then the pot has grown so large, there are so few remaining bets to call, and your opponent has become so attached to the idea of winning this pot that he probably won't be able to release his hand. With some players this is still true in more obvious cases where it should seem apparent that they must be beaten.

When playing Stud, it's often best to fire the check/raise on 5th Street. There are two reasons. First, this is the point in Stud at which the bet sizes have doubled. Second, if you waited until 6th Street, cards will sometimes fall that may scare your opponent out of betting. Then you will have missed your opportunity to gain the extra bet. Only when your hand seems very securely in the lead and your opponent appears confident should you delay your check/raise until 6th Street in Stud.

Check/Raising to Thin the Field

There is, however, a second application for the check/raise and it's probably the more useful of the two. Let's say you're playing 7 Card Stud. A deuce is forced, a 7 and a 9 limp in, then a Jack raises it and you call the raise with:

Four of you stay to see 4th Street. There, you pair your Queen and fall high on board showing a 6-Queen offsuit. If you bet here, there may be too many callers for one big pair. However, if you check, the Jack is likely to bet (since he came in raising) then you can raise, possibly driving the other two players out. Now you can go heads up with a probable pair of Jacks which is a more desirable situation for you.

On the other hand, if you had caught something like the deuce of clubs you'd be happy to just call a bet from the Jack, letting everybody else in with your four-flush. Your reason for just flat calling is that you still don't have a hand, but if you catch another club you'll most likely be able to beat everybody!

Using the check/raise to isolate yourself with one opponent is a play that should be used when you're either a modest favorite, and occasionally even a modest underdog. For example, let's say that instead of starting with the Queen-10/6 of clubs, you had:

against that same 7, the 9 and the raising Jack. Now, suppose you again caught the offsuit Queen on 4th Street, still making you high on board. You now have an underpair with two overcards to the probable pair of Jacks. Your hand is probably worse than his at the moment, but easily worth a play. The other potential callers, however, are probably eating into your winning chances more than what their extra calls are worth to you.

Why? It's true that if you catch one of your overcards on 5th Street, you'd be in pretty good shape even if the pot was still four way. But all your improvements won't be to

Kings up or Queens up. What happens if on 5th Street you catch, say, a 4? Then on 6th Street or at the river you make 6s and 4s—or catch two running 3s? Sixes up would have a fighting chance against just one player who had two Jacks on 4th Street, but would have very little chance against all three hands. There are just too many players and your hand has become strong enough to put in an extra bet if that will shake somebody loose. So if the Jack is an aggressive bettor (and the other players' boards don't look too threatening) you can check, then raise to trim the field after the Jack bets. Had the pot been just three way, you might be more prone to check and call because there's a tad less money in the pot and your hand would be a little stronger against only two opponents if it improved.

There is, however, a problem with this particular check/raise; namely, what to do on 5th Street? You're high on board and probably still don't have the best hand, though you are just a small underdog. If you bet on five, you're semi-bluffing. Yet, if you check and the Jack bets, you have a legitimate call. For these reasons, you should probably bet one more time on 5th Street to give your opponent a chance to throw his hand away. If he calls there, you can go for the free card on 6th if you still haven't improved. Of course, if you've made two pair by then, you'll just keep betting as if that's what you were going to do all along.

Concept #18: Real Bluffing Isn't Like in the Movies

Brett Maverick squeezes out his five cards, finding the 10/J/Q/K of hearts and the 7 of spades. Calling a $200 opening bet by the bad guy, Maverick draws one card while the villain draws three. The mustached villain, seeing that he caught a third Ace on the draw, brashly announces with an evil smile, "I reckon I'll bet about $500."

"That's a pretty big bet cowboy, but you and I both know it's 80-to-1 you didn't make anything better than a puny three of a kind," taunts Maverick. "So why don't we just raise it up, say, another $2000!"

The villain's smile turns to fear as he watches Maverick toss a huge stack of bills into the pot and calmly light up a stogy. "What's-a-matter?" asks Maverick. "Haven't got the cash? Shoot, I'll accept the deed to your poacher's mine as collateral if that's the problem."

The two stare each other down in silence for another minute or so, then the bad guy throws his trip Aces into the muck. "Did you have it?" asks the villain as Maverick scoops up the money. "Forgot to look. Let's find out together," quips Maverick as he flips over:

Once again, our hero runs the villain right out of the pot with a stone cold bluff. So much for the movies!

In real-life poker, bluffs are far less dramatic than in the movies and are used very sparingly. An outright, bare, naked bluff is probably attempted maybe once every 100 hands and it usually fails! Yet, bluffing does have its place in poker, although it must be used in the right spots.

What's the right spot for a bluff? Here's rule number one. Never bluff when it doesn't look like you have much. Now that may sound pathetically obvious, but it may not be. Here's an example. You're playing 7 Card Stud and start out with a split pair of 6s. After all the cards are out you end up with:

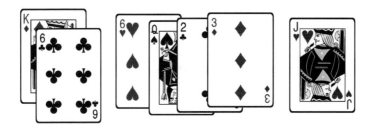

You failed to improve while your opponent now shows:

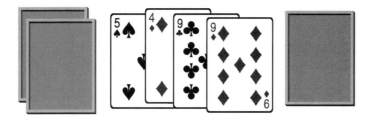

and checks on the end. If you try to bluff here, you'll most likely be called. Your board just doesn't look like anything in particular. But, if instead of having that Queen on 4th Street, you had the 7 of hearts so that your board looked like this:

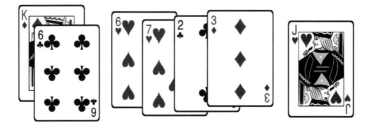

your bluff just might get your opponent to fold, fearing a straight or a flush. So before attempting an outright bluff, always ask yourself, "What does my opponent read me for?"

Also, think about the hand you're trying to bluff out. Did your opponent come into the pot raising or calling? If he entered raising, he's likely to have more than just a pair of 9s—in which case he's probably in his "check and call" mode. But if he came in calling, he may have been on a draw and you might be able to run those two 9s out of the pot.

Here's another important concept to understand about bluffing. It's easier to bluff out a good player than a bad player. Good players try to play carefully. They don't like calling when they are beat. They want to save bets. When a good player is bet into on the end, he'll review how you played the hand and try to figure out what you may have made. If your board implies a potentially good hand, your bet may get him out of there. But a bad player came to gamble. He doesn't care what your board looks like, if he's come this far, he's going to call.

Even with all these qualifications, most outright bluffs still fail to work. But that doesn't mean they should be abandoned altogether. Why not? Because they only have to work maybe 10 percent to 15 percent of the time to show a profit. Here's why:

In the 7 Stud hand illustrated above, suppose the pot was three handed up to 5th Street and then became heads up the rest of the way. Let's say the stakes were $20/$40. Counting a bet and call on every street, there would be about $300 in the pot just before your $40 bluff at the river. If you succeed in stealing that $300 just one time in eight, your combined bluffs will make money. And that's not all. Getting caught bluffing will earn you many calls in the future when you really do have the goods. It puts some deception into your play so that you won't be a "readout" at the poker table. So when considering an outright, bare naked, stone cold bluff, remember these next three tips:

1. Bluff with hands that threaten to be something serious.
2. Don't bluff into a scary-looking opposing hand.
3. Bluff against careful players who try to save bets.

Concept #19: The Art of Semi-Bluffing

You've just seen how the odds are stacked against succeeding with an outright bluff. That's why they are seldom tried. It turns out that the real value of bluffing in poker comes from something called semi-bluffing. That's when you bet or raise with only a reasonably good hand that might look better than it is, but is easy to improve. Playing this way teams together two powerful poker offensives (betting strongly combined with the chance of making a good hand). As a result, semi-bluffing gives you more ways to win the pot than if you'd played your hand passively.

Picture yourself starting out a Stud hand with a pair of red 3s in the hole and the King of spades up. A deuce brings it in, then a 10 raises and you call. The deuce now folds and you are left alone in there with the raiser who possibly has a pair of 10s. Next, you buy the Queen of spades and being high, but having only a pair of 3s you check, as does your opponent, who caught a 6. On 5th Street, you catch a Jack of spades while your opponent makes an open pair of 6s and bets them. You call. Here's how the situation looks thus far:

Your Hand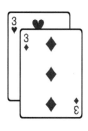

Opponent s Hand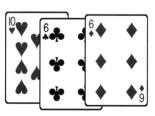

Have you noticed what's happened here? Because of the way you've played up to now, about the only way you can win this pot is to make the winning hand. That's because you never gave your opposition particular reason to fear you even though you had a playable hand and a fearsome board. But let's flash back to the beginning of the hand to see if you could have helped things to turn out any differently.

On the first three cards, when the deuce brought it in and the 10 raised, if you had re-raised would the 10 have even called, looking at a King? Probably, but maybe not. This could have been a chance to steal the pot early. If he does call, though, he's probably playing in fear of your King. That's important.

Now, when you catch the suited Queen on the turn, if you bet right out, would the 10/6 have called there? Quite possibly not; yet another chance to win the pot without having the best hand. But if he did call again, when you proceeded to buy the Jack of spades on 5th Street would your opponent have bet his open pair of 6s? Very unlikely. Think about how scary your board would now look since you'd been raising and betting all the way.

Let's suppose your opponent did check his 6s to you. Should you bet even though your hand is beaten in sight? Positively! Why? First of all, because your opponent may very well fold, fearing a myriad of strong hands judging by the appearance of your board. But if he does call, and your sixth card is any Ace, King, Queen, Jack, 10, or spade (more than half the remaining deck), your opponent almost can't call unless he has a pretty big hand himself. And if your sixth card is a blank, he'll probably still check to you. But if he does bet, you have enough potential to call even if you're sure he already has 10s and 6s.

Notice that because of the cards you caught, and the way you bet them, your opponent was liable to give up his hand on any street. The moral to this story is—if you start out with a hand that's worth playing and looks formidable, semi-bluffing is often better than just calling for three reasons:

1. Your opponent may choose not to get involved in an expensive pot.
2. You may catch intimidating cards that will drive the opposition out later.
3. You may actually make the winning hand.

If you just check and call, you cannot win via numbers 1 or 2. You need to give yourself those extra ways of winning the pot and semi-bluffing provides them. Don't get carried away with this tactic, however, and become overaggressive. Semi-bluffing isn't something that should be done every time you have a playable second best hand. If you do it habitually, your opponents will begin to disregard your "unimpressive" raises and play right through you. So pick your hands and pick your opponents selectively!

Chapter 4

Pot Odds

To win at poker, you have to be able to determine what's worth the risk and what's not. Many of these determinations have to be made during the heat of the hand. Sometimes it's wrong to try for an open-end straight, and sometimes it's right go for the inside straight, even though a straight would win the pot in both spots! The thing that makes it right or wrong is your *pot odds*.

Concept #20: You Need Higher Pot Odds Than Your Odds Against Winning

Suppose you're playing 5 Card Draw poker at the country club with a bunch of zillionaires, Jacks or Better to open. Six players ante a $20 bill each, you can open for $100 and bet $200 after the draw. Everybody checks around to you. Squeezing out your hand, you find:

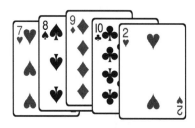

You have an open-end straight draw and must check also since you don't have openers. The player right behind you is dead last to act and opens for $100, meaning he must have Jacks or better. One by one, everybody folds until it's just the opener and you. You should fold, too! Why? Because if you call and draw one card, you'll make your straight only one time in six. And when you do, you'll have to make back all the money you lost the other five times you missed, or you're playing a losing game of poker.

Here's how that works. It'll cost you $100 to draw to your straight. Let's assume that if you make it, you'll win the $120 that was already in the ante, plus your opponent's $100 opening bet, plus a $200 call from him after the draw (maybe). That's a potential gain of $420 the one time out of six that you make your hand. But you'll lose $100 each of those other five times you miss for $500 in losses and will be a net loser over-all. Simple enough. It's not that you should never draw to an open end straight in poker. It's just that in this particular situation *you are not getting the proper pot odds to do so* because you were only getting a little over 4-to-1 pot odds on a 5-to-1 shot.

Now let's look at a situation that stacks up a little differently. Say you're in a $30/$60 Seven Card Stud hand at one of the local casinos. Originally, the pot was four-way action, but by 6th Street you're in there all alone with one opponent who is showing:

 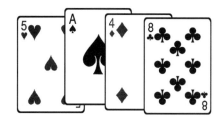

As he bets $60, he accidentally flashes his hole cards revealing a 6 and a 7 for an 8 high straight. You have Q-Q/9-K-10-3. Due to all the earlier betting the pot already contains $600. This time it's definitely correct to call and try for the inside Jack at the river. If you hit it, you'll collect 11- or 12-to-1 on a 9-to-1 shot. Now you've got yourself an overlay (inside straight draws are normally 11-to-1 against, but in this illustration 12 cards have been eliminated, yet no Jacks).

That is how the concept of pot odds works. Pay attention to them. At the end of your poker life, much of your net result will be made up of a blend of all the pot odds you were receiving along the way. If your pot odds were always higher than your odds against winning the pot, there's bound to be some chips left over after making all those calls. But if your odds against winning were higher than the payoff odds the pot was offering you, then you'll end up making up the difference from your stack and that's a losing game.

Concept #21: Your Pot Odds Are Not Always What They Seem

Whenever there's just one more card to come in a poker hand, as in the previous concept, your pot odds are easy to figure. All you need to do is divide the cost of the bet into the size of the eventual pot, then measure those odds against your odds to make the winning hand. For example, suppose you're going to the river in a Hold'em hand with a pair of 10s in the pocket and the board is:

You've just lost "overpair" status when that Ace fell on the turn and the recent betting convinces you that your pocket 10s are no longer any good. But all is not completely lost because an inside 7 will make you a straight (for purposes of this illustration, we'll ignore the two extra "outs" you might win with if a 10 comes). Since a "gut shot" (inside) straight draw in this spot is about 10-to-1 against, you'll need to make a profit of at least 10 times the cost of calling to see the river card, or you should fold. So if the bet is $60, the eventual pot will have to be at least $600 (not counting your own call) to make it worthwhile going for. That's fairly straight forward.

But what about when you're on 5th Street in a 7 Stud hand with two more cards to come as in the example below?

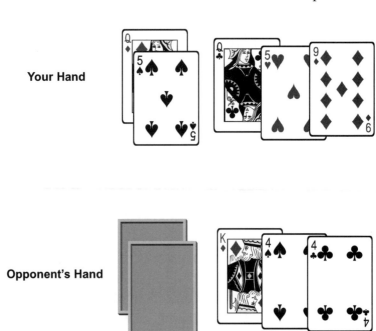

Your Hand

Opponent's Hand

According to the way the hands were bet, you are almost positive your opponent now has Kings up. You'll need to fill up to win, about a 5-to-1 shot. The bet is $60 and it looks like the pot will contain maybe $600 at the river. That's around 9-to-1 (10-*for*-1) on your $60. Should you call? The answer is no. Why? Because getting to the river will cost not one—but two bets, or $120. And if you figured that $600 pot would also contain your river bet, then $180 of it would be your own money. So you'd net only $420 while risking $120 to try for your full house. That's 3.5-to-1 pot odds! The lesson here is that when there are multiple cards yet to come and *you need to add up all those calls*, then compare that cost to your anticipated net profit on the hand (remember not to add your own future calls into the size of the pot). And by the way; if you're also planning to call at the river even if you miss just to keep him honest, then your odds become $420 to $180— less than 2.5-to-1!

Actually, in the example just given, things are even a little worse for you, since your opponent will occasionally fill up too. In reality, you're about a 6-to-1 dog here to make a full house and still win the pot. So you'd need to net over $700, not counting your own two calls on 5th and 6th Streets, assuming you fold if you miss. That would require about a $900 final pot. You will be very seldom getting that kind of price and that is why you've almost always got to fold in that situation.

Concept #22: Cutting Down Your Opponent's Pot Odds

Whenever you can call a bet getting higher pot odds than your odds against winning the pot, you've got an odds "overlay" and should play onward. However, the same goes for your opponent. Fortunately, many times you can alter an opponent's pot odds for the worse.

Recognizing all the times it's right to do this is a tricky matter that depends upon many factors. However, there are two situations in which you should typically raise to cut down your opponent's pot odds. The first is when you're in a three-way pot and don't really know whether you have the bettor beaten, but you're almost sure you're better than the second opponent. Here's a typical example from $20/$40 Texas Hold'em.

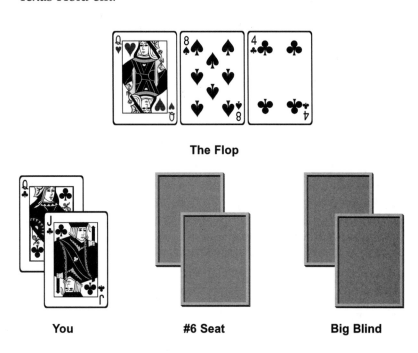

The Flop

You   **#6 Seat**   **Big Blind**

The #6 seat raised it to $40 before the flop, then you called from the #8 seat and so did the big blind. On the flop, the big blind checked and the #6 seat bet $20. You've got top pair with a questionable kicker. If the #6 seat came in raising with A/A, K/K, A/Q, or K/Q he has you in terrible shape. On the other hand, if he has A/K, A/J, or pocket Jacks, 10s or 9s you are in the driver's seat. So maybe you have the best hand and maybe you don't.

But what about the big blind? There are lots of second-class hands he might have called a single raise with before the flop. While you probably have him beaten, he could have flopped something like a pair of 8s with 7/8 or 8/9, a gut shot straight draw with 9/10, 10/J, 5/6, or 6/7—or maybe he has a back-door flush draw and an overcard with a suited Ace. All these hands would require fairly high pot odds for him to keep coming. There would be $170 in the pot right after you called and he'd be getting over 8-to-1 momentary odds, a good enough price for most of those hands. But if you raised it to $40, the big blind would then be getting less than 5-to-1 ($190 to $40) and should probably fold.

In those kinds of spots, raising just costs you more money when you don't have the best hand and helps you the times you do. But overall, raising helps more than it hurts because of its potential to move somebody with an otherwise playable hand right out of the picture—so raise you must!

The second spot in which you should just about always raise to cut down somebody's pot odds is when it looks as if you probably have a small but delicate lead in a multi-way hand. Here's an example from a $20/$40 Seven Card Stud hand (see following page).

A deuce brought it in and you immediately raised with split Jacks. The Queen flat called and then the King re-popped it to $40. Both you and the Queen called the King's re-raise. You were prepared to fold on 5th Street, but instead you made concealed Jacks and 10s there. The King bets with a probable pair of Kings and might even possibly have concealed Kings up or trips (normally one combined chance in five or six). Still, you should raise to cut down the Queen's pot odds. If he folds you gain a lot, since he would have been your demise whenever he makes Queens up and the Kings don't improve. Even if the Queen doesn't fold, you've forced him to pay extra to chase you which accrues to your advantage; not as much as driving him out, but you gain equity either way.

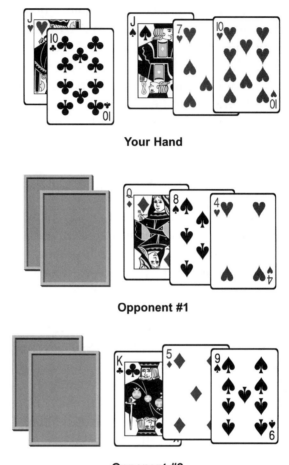

Your Hand

Opponent #1

Opponent #2

Concept #23: When NOT to Cut Down Your Opponent's Pot Odds

Some very aggressive players go too far with raising in order to blow the third man out of the pot. If that third player has too small a chance to draw out considering his pot odds, and a raise will drive him out, you are better off letting him in for one bet. This can easily occur when you have the second best hand in a three-way pot as in the 7 Stud example below.

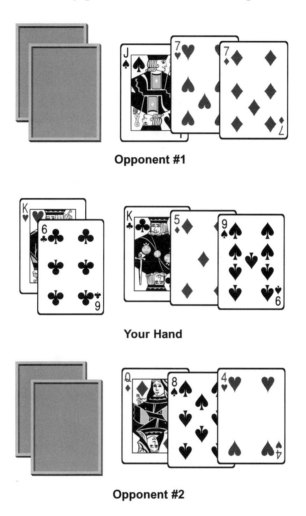

Opponent #1

Your Hand

Opponent #2

This is similar to the previous situation, except this time you have the two Kings and the probable Jacks has made an open pair. Since he is now high on board and figures to have the best hand, he bets. Contrary to the way many aggressive players play, you should just call here. There are a few spots where you should raise without having the best hand, but this isn't one of them. The Queen is actually subsidizing your position and you don't want him to go away, because with or without him, you need to make a second pair and if you do, your Kings up will probably beat both opponents!

Concept #24: Good Pots Odds Doesn't Mean You Can Play a Bad Hand

There's a very common misunderstanding about pot odds and weak hands. The mistake is thinking that lots of callers give you a good enough price to trail in with an inferior hand. With special types of hands this can be true, but shabby hands in general should never be played regardless of how many callers there are. A concise example comes from Texas Hold'em.

Let's say the numbers 3, 5, 7, and 8 seats all flat call and you're sitting on the button with:

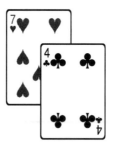

You think to yourself, "Hmm, look at the odds I'm getting on my money, let me in there." Bad move! Here's why. Let's just say that the first four players have something moderate like:

#3 seat	Q/J
#5 seat	8/8
#7 seat	K/10
#8 seat	A/9 suited

Since nobody raised, you can get in for just one bet, so you call with your weakstick 7/4. The small blind then folds and the big blind checks with 5/3. With six-way action you'll be getting about 5-to-1 on your initial call. So how big a dog do you think you are to win the pot? You're a 9-to-1 shot!

Surprised? It should make sense when you think about it, since the average holding must have about one chance in six if it's a six-way pot. The weaker your hand is, the worse your chances get. It's true that as more players come in your pot odds go up, but with all those hands to beat your odds against winning go up just as fast. So the weakest hand is never getting a pot odds overlay—*unless it's a drawing hand*, in which case it's not really the weakest hand. It's important to recognize that the main reason you play a drawing hand, whenever you play it, is to make a straight or a flush. Either it develops quickly or you get away from it. If it does bloom, you've got a big hand that can usually beat a multitude of opponents. That's why you look for good pot odds with drawing hands.

But a pure trash hand such as a 7/4 offsuit in Hold'em doesn't have that kind of potential. Most often it'll miss completely or get you into trouble by flopping a 7 or a 4. Statistically, you'll flop two pair (7s and 4s) or better with it one time out of 24 and win maybe 15 bets when your hand is good. There's a losing play for you! Now, if your 7/4 were a 7/6 suited, you might want to take a shot. Then you'd flop either a straight, an open-ender, a flush, a flush draw, two pair, trips, or a full house about one time in four.

The same principle applies when you're tempted to come into a four- or five-way Stud pot with a piece o' cheese like 3-6/6. With so many players, two small pair, if you make them, are just going to cost you money, so what are you trying to make? You'd be better off seeing 4th Street with a 7-9/10 if the 6s, 8s, 10s, and Jacks are live. You either catch something interesting right on the turn or you are done with it.

Good pot odds can make non-premium drawing hands worth taking a shot with on the chance that you snag a card that will give you a premium drawing hand. But as for those run-of-the-mill trash hands, leave them in the muck where they belong.

Concept #25: Figuring Your Pot Odds in Split Pot Games

Whenever you are considering your pot odds to determine whether to continue playing, you probably don't have the best hand. There's a certain advantage in that. The advantage is if you don't improve, you usually won't have to call a bet at the river. As a result, when you are chasing you are often getting better pot odds than the leader in the hand since you'll usually save the last bet when you miss. This factor does funny things to your pot odds in split pot games.

For example, if you are going to the river in a "high only" game and you're a 4-to-1 shot to make the nuts, but will get 8-to-1 odds from the pot if you hit, you should go for it. That's easy. But how about in high/low split? There, you'd get only half the pot. In that exact same situation you should probably fold because getting 8-to-1 when you win the whole pot typically boils down to getting only about 3-to-1 when you have to split it. To see how this works, let's look at an unusually clear-cut $50/$100 Omaha high/low split example. Suppose you're in a three-way pot and you hold:

and on 4th Street the board is:

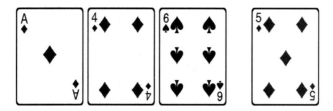

There's a bet and a call and now it's up to you. With the low virtually certain and both straights and flushes very likely, you need to make Aces full to win half and have nine live cards to do it with—one Ace, three 4s, two 6s and three 5s out of 44 unseen cards. That makes you just about a 4-to-1 shot. The pot contains $600 thus far. If you call (bringing the current pot to $700) and miss at the river, you'll fold losing just $100. If you fill up, counting your river bet and a $100 call from each of the other two players (with no raises), there will be $1,000 in the pot when it's over. If you'd have won it all, you'd have netted 8-to-1 pot odds on your $100 4th Street call. But when you win only half, you'll get back just $500. After subtracting your own money, you'll have made only $300 profit, or 3-to-1 pot odds. And since you are a 4-to-1 underdog to fill, you should just fold your three Aces on the turn.

If the pot were four-way action, you might get paid off somewhat better, but either way, you'd need to get in some raises and split a $1,400 pot to make playing worthwhile ($700 for your half, minus the $300 you put into it). This example highlights the fact that when you are drawing to half the pot, several situations that may seem like an automatic call aren't really worth it because *when the pot will be split, you're getting less than half the net pot odds than if you won the whole pot.*

Part of the reason why is because 8-*to*-1 is really 9-*for*-1 and half of that is 4.5-*for*-1 which is 3.5-*to*-1. But those proportions get knocked even further out of kilter when you fold at the river if you miss. Calculating this out at the table is not something you want to mess with during the heat of the hand. What you need at a time like that is a handy short cut to indicate your play. That's what the following table is for. In most situations, your pot odds relative to scooping vs. splitting will usually break down just about like this:

When You Scoop	When You Split
6 to 1	2 to 1
8 to 1	3 to 1
10 to 1	4 to 1
12 to 1	5 to 1

As you can see, your "split" odds are less than half your "scoop" odds. Notice that you can just cut your "scoop" odds in half and subtract one to get your "split" odds. So here's what you do. When judging whether to continue on for a split, look at the pot and estimate it's probable eventual size. Then say to yourself, "If I could win it all, I'd be getting about 8-to-1 pot odds, therefore I'm getting about 3-to-1 for half. Am I worse than a 3-to-1 dog?" If the answer is yes, fold; if not, call!

Concept #26: The Odds of Improving Your Hand

Following is a chart that tells you in practical terms how big a favorite or underdog you are to improve your hand in the popular casino poker games. It's a workman's guide. Rather than split hairs and state that you're a 31.4 percent shot to make a straight when you flop an open-ender in Hold'em, the chart just says you're a 2-to-1 underdog, although you're actually a 2.18-to-1 dog. I find the round numbers to be a usable tool at the table where exact percentages become both confusing and superfluous.

Most key situations that you'll run into during a hand have been included. Getting a good feel for their odds can be of considerable help when deciding how, or whether to play your hand.

7 Card Stud Odds

Hand on 3rd Street	Finish With (or better)	Approximate Odds
one pair	two pair	1.5-to-1 favorite
trips	full house	1.5-to-1 underdog
three-flush	flush	4.5-to-1 underdog
three-straight	straight	5-to-1 underdog
three to an 8 low	8 low	even money
three to a 7 low	7 low	2-to-1 underdog
on 5th Street		
one pair	two pair	9-to-8 underdog
two pair	full house	5-to-1 underdog
trips	full house	2-to-1 underdog
four-flush	flush	2-to-1 underdog
open-ender	straight	2-to-1 underdog
gut-shot	straight	5-to-1 underdog
four to an 8 low	8 low	4-to-3 favorite
three to an 8 low	8 low	6-to-1 underdog
four to a 7 low	7 low	6-to-5 underdog

Hold'em Odds

Hole Cards	Chance to Flop	Approximate Odds
a pair	trips (or better)	7.5-to-1 underdog
A/K	top pair (or better)	*2.5-to-1 underdog
K/Q	top pair	3-to-1 underdog
7/4	two pair (or better)	23-to-1 underdog
suited hand	flush	118-to-1 underdog
suited hand	flush draw	8-to-1 underdog
7/8, 8/9, 9/10, etc.	straight	75-to-1 underdog
7/8, 8/9, 9/10, etc.	straight draw	9-to-1 underdog
7/8, 8/9, 9/10, etc.	gut-shot draw	4.5-to-1 underdog

*does not include those times which you make top pair but there's another pair on board such as with A-9-9 or Q-8-5-A-8

On the Flop:

Hole Cards	Flop Is	Finish With	Approximate Odds
A/K	J-8-5	top pair or better	*4-to-1 underdog
A/K suited	J-8-5 w/ flush draw	top pair or flush	even money
J/9	J-A-5	Js & 9s or better	4-to-1 underdog
J/9	10-7-2	straight	4.5-to-1 underdog
J/9	10-8-2	straight	2-to-1 underdog
J/9 suited	flush draw	flush	2-to-1 underdog
J/9 suited	one flush card	flush	23-to-1 underdog
J/9 suited	10-8-2 w/ flush draw	straight or flush	6-to-5 favorite

Omaha Odds

Hole Cards	Chance to Flop	Approximate Odds
A-2-Q-K	nut low	13-to-1 underdog
A-2-Q-K	nut low draw	2-to-1 underdog
A-2-Q-K	nut low or nut draw	1.5-to-1 underdog
A-2-3-K	nut low	7-to-1 underdog
A-2-3-K	nut low draw	4-to-3 underdog
A-2-3-K	nut low or nut draw	6-to-5 favorite

On the Flop:

Hole Cards	Flop Is	Finish With	Approximate Odds
A-2-Q-K	7-8-9	nut low	even money
A-2-Q-K	8-9-10	nut low	5-to-1 underdog
A-2-Q-K	6-7-8	counterfeited	3-to-1 underdog
A-2-3-K	7-8-9	nut low	2.25-to-1 favorite
A-2-3-K	8-9-10	nut low	3-to-1 underdog
A-2-3-K	6-7-8	dbl. counterfeited	36-to-1 underdog

*does not include those times which you make top pair but there's another pair on board such as with A-9-9 or Q-8-5-A-8

Section B

Strategy for Specific Games

Chapter 5

7 Card Stud

7 Card Stud is the old mainstay of public poker rooms. The lowest stakes game in the house is generally 7 Stud. That's because rank beginners are usually familiar with it, where they may never have played games such as Hold'em or Omaha.

Casino 7 Card Stud is played just about the same as it would be on your kitchen table among family members, except for the following three fine points:

1. The low card on 3rd Street must start the action by being forced in for a small bet.
2. The betting stakes double on 5th Street with no under-betting allowed.
3. An open pair on 4th Street may bet the smaller or the larger amount.

With all that remaining constant from one Stud game to the next, there's still one inside factor that varies from game to game as the stakes rise and fall, and that is:

Concept #27: The Ante Structure

The ante in a $15/$30 Stud game is $2 per player. That's one-fifteenth of the betting limit. However, as the stakes get richer, the ante gets richer even faster. At $80/$160 Stud, for example, the ante is $20 per player. That's one-eighth of the betting limit, or nearly twice as rich proportionally as the $15/$30 game! Games between these two levels generally have antes structured somewhere between those two ratios (i.e.—at $30/$60 Stud the ante is $5, or one-twelfth the betting limit).

How does this variable affect you as a player? Here's how. The lower stakes games are geared more towards tight play. The higher games are geared for loose play. This all makes sense once you get to know Stud poker more intimately. Lesser experienced players with fewer maneuvers in their arsenals just get themselves into trouble with marginal hands. For them, the best play is to fold a marginal holding. A Stud expert, however, can take that same marginal hand and outplay his opponents with it, often turning a profit. Hence, the better you know how to play Stud, *the more hands you can play*. And since the better players usually play in the higher games, the ante structure in those higher games is appropriately richer.

If you stand on the rail and watch a $15/$30 Stud game and then walk over to an $80/$160 game, you'll see this difference in living color. In the first game, after everybody has anted $2 and the low card is forced to "bring it in" for $5, the pot contains $21. If you have something like:

and want to raise, you'll bring it to $15. If everybody folds, you'll win 7-5 odds on your money. Now if that was an $80/$160 game, you'd be putting an $80 raise into a $180 pot. If you steal that one you'll get over 2-1 odds! With such different mutuels, you just might fold those 7s in a $15/$30 game, and maybe raise with them in an $80/$160 game.

By the same token, however, your opponents would be getting better pot odds to call in the higher game, so they won't give you the pot as easily as they might concede in a smaller game. As a result, higher stakes Stud games are played looser and more aggressively than at lower limits. Again, I'll stress that this is appropriate because players at the higher levels are generally more adept at handling the faster action.

As you step up in stakes, you're going to have to learn to play a few hands you'd have folded in a smaller game. If you don't, the proportionally richer antes and the aggressive competition will gradually drain you. If that style of play takes you out of your comfort zone, look for smaller ante games near the limits you can handle.

The table below shows nearly every Stud game from $15/$30 to $80/$160 along with it's ante, bring-in and the money odds you'd be getting if you won the pot with a raise on 3rd Street. That final column is your indicator of how aggressively the game is likely to be played. (Note: $40/$80 Stud on the East Coast is generally played with a $5 ante and is often squeaky tight. $40/$80 Stud in Las Vegas and California usually has a $10 ante and plenty of action.)

Stakes	Ante	Bring-In	Odds
$15/$30	$2	$5	7-to-5
$20/$40	$3	$5	7-to-5
$30/$60	$5	$10	8-to-5
$40/$80	$5	$10	6-to-5
$40/$80	$10	$10	11-to-5
$50/$100	$10	$15	9-to-5
$60/$120	$10	$20	8-to-5
$75/$150	$15	$25	9-to-5
$80/$160	$20	$20	11-to-5

Concept #28: Playable Starting Hands

So what's a playable starting hand for 7 Card Stud? Wow! That's a question that may never be answered fully. It's a question that raises countless other questions. What's the ante structure? How many callers are there? How live is your hand? Was there a raise? Is the raiser a stronger or weaker player than you are? What upcards are behind you? Is the game tight or loose, passive or aggressive? All these things and more can affect your decision to either play or fold.

But we have to narrow things down, so let's get more specific. Probably the bottom 70 percent of all the three-card hands you'll be dealt should be mucked every time. The other 30 percent, you'll play *some of the time*. A list of potentially playable starting hands follows in order of preference. Some you'll always play, some you'll often play and some you'll play only if nearly everything's right.

1. **rolled up Trips**
2. **any pair of Aces**
3. **any pair of Kings or Queens**
4. **high three-flush**
5. **split Jacks or 10s with overcard**
6. **buried Jacks or 10s**
7. **split Jacks or 10s with undercard**
8. **split 9s or lower with overcard**
9. **high three-straight**
10. **low three-flush**
11. **buried 9s or lower**
12. **low three-straight**
13. **split 9s or lower with undercard**
14. **three high cards, 10 or higher**
15. **two-suited skip-straight**

There's not much else you'd ever want to put money into the pot with, and many of the above hands you'd need extenuating circumstances to play. Let's look at them one at a time.

1. Rolled up Trips: A 424-to-1 rarity. Whether to come in raising or calling depends upon whether you'll kill the action by raising. I'd generally raise with rolled up 10s, Jacks, or Queens because my hand looks like a big pair, but a beatable one. With smaller roll-ups, you want to look at the upcards behind you and who is holding them. If tight players have the big upcards, you might just limp in so as not to drive everybody out. If more aggressive types have the big cards, you may want to come in raising since it's more likely you'll get re-raised. Percentage of times you'll play your roll up is virtually 100 percent.

2. Pair of Aces: Another virtually "always play" start. The difference here is that you should nearly always come in raising or re-raising. You might occasionally consider just calling somebody else's raise if your Aces are buried and it looks like a shorthanded pot, but be careful, two Aces are a very beatable hand. Initial playing frequency will be about 99 percent.

3. Pair of Kings or Queens: Play these similar to the Aces, except if you get re-raised by a live overcard you'll have to start making judgments about the playing style of the re-raiser. Don't fall in love with your big pair. As soon as you are sure you are second best, muck the hand unless the pot has already gotten too big. Initial playing frequency is about 95 percent.

4. High Three-Flush: Because of its versatile potential, a hand like the Ace/Queen/9 of clubs is a strong starting hand. It can be weakened by the presence of Aces, Queens or more than two clubs on the board but, usually, you almost have to see 5th Street with this hand. If your Ace or Queen is up, and is high on board, you should probably come in raising. If an overcard already raised, you might only call. Initial playing frequency is about 95 percent.

5. Split Jacks or 10s with overcard: "Overcard" means higher than the upcard of the raiser, or higher than all but one of the upcards behind you when there's been no raise. If that's the case, your hand is quite strong and quite playable at the moment, and should probably be played aggressively. Initial playing frequency is about 90 percent.

6. Buried Jacks or 10s: Here the strength of your starting hand begins to drop off quickly. A key strength is that your pair is buried. If your upcard is higher than any other active player, however, your hand is much stronger and should be initially played as though you had that particular split pair. In contrast, you might want to fold buried 10s or Jacks with a low upcard if a tight player showing an overcard to your Jacks has raised. Overall initial playing frequency is about 85 percent.

7. Split Jacks or 10s with undercard: You should come in raising if there's been no raise and there are no more than two overcards behind you. If the overcards behind you are very aggressive players, however, you'll want to consider how far you can go with this hand. The smaller the ante, the deader your cards, the more players in the hand, and the less experienced you are, the more likely you should fold. Initial playing frequency is 75 to 80 percent.

8. Split 9s or lower with overcard: The overcard is the key to making a medium or small pair playable. If the overcard's an Ace or a boss King (boss King means there's no Ace anywhere on the board, so your King is a "boss" kicker), and all five of your "improvement" cards are live, you can normally raise or call a raise and probably go at least to 5th Street. With a Queen overcard kicker, you have to be leery of an Ace or King that might fall later. That's where a pair of 9s would be more playable than something like a pair of 5s. Initial playing frequency is about 80 percent.

9. High Three-Straight: Hands such as 10/Jack/Queen or Jack/Queen/King are stronger if their top card and the card just above it are completely live. But if they're not and a King or an Ace comes in raising you may want to give it up. Overall initial playing frequency is about 75 percent.

10. Low Three-Flush: With no high cards to pair, the biggest key is that your flush draw is live. If more than one spade is out, you should fold something like the 4/7/10 of spades in the typical scenario where a picture card raises and the pot is going to be two- or three-handed. Initial playing frequency is about 60 percent.

11. Buried pair of 9s or lower: Your upcard kicker here is of paramount importance. If it is big and your hand is live, you can usually play somewhat aggressively. If it is small and dead with big cards raising, plus your buried pair is small, fold. Overall initial playing frequency is 50 to 60 percent.

12. Low Three-Straight: Hands like 5/6/7 must have their 4s and 8s very live as well as your door card so that you might "bet and take it" by making an open pair on 4th Street. The live 3s and 9s are also of secondary "straighting" importance, since you don't know which way you may need to go if you improve on 4th Street. Even then, if the pot is heads-up these starting hands are a poor value. Initial playing frequency is 40 to 50 percent.

13. Split 9s or lower with undercard: With no decent kicker, you're going pretty much on the strength of your split pair alone. Nines are a lot more playable than 5s and your pair must be completely live. Even then, you probably shouldn't call a raise from an overcard, and should fold even if there's been no raise when there are three high cards behind you. Initial playing frequency is 35 to 40 percent.

14. Three High Cards, 10 or higher: If a King or Queen is raising and you hold Ace/Queen/10, your hand has very poor value. But if there was no raise yet, and you are in a late seat and your hand is live, you can raise representing a big pair. Initial playing frequency is about 33 percent.

15. Two-suited Skip-Straight: Hands like 8/10/Jack with two hearts can be played in high-ante multi-way pots when the 9s, Jacks, Queens, and hearts are pretty live and you can get in for just the first raise. Other than that, they should usually be mucked. Initial playing frequency is about 25 percent.

Concept #29: The Value of Overcards

When you start out with a pair in 7 Card Stud, the size of your kicker is key. A starting pair of Queens is about a 2-to-1 favorite over a starting pair of Jacks, if both players have smaller kickers. If the Queen came in raising, and you know this is a tight player who almost has to have the two Queens to do this, you should fold your Jacks. But in the following scenario:

Hand #1

Hand #2

the pair of Jacks is only a 7-to-5 underdog due to his overcard kicker. Now, because of the pot odds created by the antes and the low card bring-in, the Jacks are well worth playing, unless a couple of Kings and/or Jacks are dead. In fact, if your pair of Jacks was buried with the overcard kicker exposed—like this:

your hand would be even stronger for two reasons. Yes, you'd still be a 7-to-5 underdog to beat the Queens if you both played to the river. But if you re-raised right here, the Queens may not play to the river, fearing that you have a pair of Kings. That's how an overcard door card can be used to intimidate. If he does stay with you, your hand is worth taking to the river anyway on the sheer value of that overcard, unless the Queen catches other ominous cards later in the hand. The second advantage is if you happen to hit a Jack, the Queens will have no way of knowing that you've just made trips. For these reasons, when you figure you have an under-pair to the raiser, a good strategy is generally to:

1. **Fold if your kicker is smaller than the raiser's door card.**
2. **Call if you have an overcard kicker in the hole.**
3. **Re-raise if you have a buried pair with an overcard door card.**

Concept #30: Second Best on 3rd Street

It was just mentioned that if you can determine that you have the second best pair on 3rd Street, you should fold right there unless you have an overcard kicker. Mathematically, this is true. The problem is, sometimes you don't find out you have the second best pair until too many raises have been put into the pot. If more than five total bets went in on 3rd Street, even if you are positive you have Kings to his Aces, you're going to have to play the hand because of the high pot odds that everybody has just created.

Let's say the scenario goes like this: You're playing $30/$60 where the ante is the typical $5 per player. The low card comes in for $10 and a Queen immediately raises it to $30. You re-pop it to $60 with split Kings and then a tight player with an Ace up makes it $90 and the Queen gets out, figuring he's beaten in two spots. Even though you're almost certainly against split Aces, six bets have already gone into the pot right here. That makes it wrong to give up your hand even though you're a 2-to-1 underdog. Had the betting just gone $10-$30-$60, you should fold if you are virtually sure you are beat. But those extra few bets give you the right price to continue playing because the pot already contains $230 and your opponent figures to put in another $150 by the time you reach the river. On your end, you'll put in $180 counting your call on 3rd Street. That gives you pot odds of 380-180 not including any river bets which you'll get the lion's share of, since you most likely won't call a bet on the end with just one pair.

So when six bets go into the pot on 3rd Street, your proper strategy is to play to the river with the second best pair—with or without an overcard—as long as your hand remains fairly live and your opponent doesn't make an open pair. Even at 5th Street you should continue under these circumstances. If the pot contains any fewer than six bets (plus the antes) on 3rd Street, fold the second best pair with no overcard—unless your opponent has shown that he'll play a big three-flush or a small, buried pair with an Ace kicker the same way he would a pair of split Aces.

Concept #31: Stud Is a "Live Card" Game

The title to this concept cannot be overstressed. Just about every starting hand below #3 in Concept #28 is heavily dependent upon how live it is and how live it remains as the hand plays out. In fact, if you insist on trying to make hands in this game when your cards are dead, then Stud poker just isn't going to be your game. Hand #4 from Concept #28 is illustrated below as an example:

If an Ace comes in raising, then a Queen calls and there are four other clubs on board this hand is almost useless. In this spot you'll make a flush only one time out of 11 if you go all the way. Besides that, it's fair to guess that either the Ace or the Queen has a split pair. If just one of them does, you wouldn't be that likely to improve your hand at all by 5th Street—and many of your improvements will just cost you more money. Here you really ought to throw your big three-flush away.

Now, instead, if there was only one other club on board, you'd make your flush one time in five. If at the same time there were no Aces, Queens or 9s showing you'd then be a 5-to-2 favorite to improve in some way by 5th Street. Now your big three-flush is actually pretty potent. The "liveness" of your hand on 3rd Street strongly affects your ability to either catch cards, or not be able to complete a hand. As another example, let's look at starting hand #11 from Concept #28:

If a 7 and a 4 are out, and a Queen came in raising, your hand is a "piece-o'-cheese" and you should fold. You'll have a tough time making even two small pair. But instead if you held:

and the 5s, 6s, 7s, 8s, and clubs were fairly live while that same Queen came in raising, you'd want to take at least one card off, maybe two. In this spot your hand is much stronger, since many more cards will develop your hand.

Both of these last two examples were shown at their extremes so that you can clearly see how much difference the liveness of your hand can make. Always consider these factors before deciding whether to play your hand as well as how to play it.

Concept #32: "Live Card" Hand Odds

We were just discussing in the previous concept that if you start with a three-flush and four of your suit are out, you'll make a flush only once in eleven tries if you play to the river. The table below shows your improvement odds (for the end of the hand) for various three-card starting hands depending upon how live your cards are on 3rd Street in an eight-handed game. This will give you an idea of how dead cards hurt your chances to improve. In general, you probably shouldn't play if as many as 20 percent of your "helping" cards are dead on 3rd Street.

You Have: Three Spades

Spades Out	Make Flush
0	3-to-1 against
1	4-to-1 against
2	5-to-1 against
3	7-to-1 against
4	10-to-1 against

You Have: 9/10/J

8s & Qs out	Make Straight
0	3-to-1 against
1	4-to-1 against
2	5-to-1 against
3	6-to-1 against
4	7-to-1 against

You Have: A/6/6

Aces & 6s out	Make Aces Up or Better
0	3-to-2 against
1	2-to-1 against
2	3-to-1 against

You Have: 7/6/6 with two clubs

5s, 6s, 7s 8s, and clubs out	Make Aces Up or Better
0	2-to-1 against
3	5-to-2 against
6	3-to-1 against

You Have: 3/6/6 unsuited

3s & 6s out	Make Aces Up or Better
0	5-to-2 against
1	3-to-1 against
2	7-to-2 against

You Have: 7/9/10 with two clubs

7s, 8s, 9s, 10s, and clubs out	Make Aces Up or Better
0	11-to-5 against
3	3-to-1 against
6	7-to-2 against

Concept #33: Beware the Paired Door Card

Suppose you start out a $30/$60 Stud hand with a split pair of Jacks and raise it to $30 coming in. A player with a 10 show- ing calls your raise, and by 5th Street the situation looks like this (see following page):

Now, falling high on board, the pair of 10s bets $60. Everyone else folds and it is up to you. One of the most dan- gerous things that can happen in a 7 Stud hand is when your opponent pairs his "door card" as he has here. Why? Because of all the hands a responsible player would come into a pot with, a healthy chunk of those would be a pair of whatever his door card is. And when he pairs that card on board, he may very well have made trips. It wouldn't be nearly as dan- gerous if your opponent's board read 6-10-10.

Your Hand

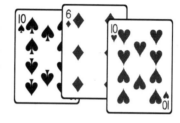

Opponent's Hand

Notice however, that I said, a "responsible" player. If your opponent is a loose, wild gambler who plays lots of hands, then a paired door card doesn't tell you a whole lot. But most poker players who have been through the school of hard knocks require some legitimate value in their three-card starting hands before they'll put money into the pot.

Let's say your opponent in the scenario above is a typical veteran who wouldn't have played with anything less than a pair, a three-flush or a three-straight. This is a reasonable assumption. Then based upon the random distribution of those poker hands, for every 20 times he pairs his door card he'll have:

trips	**8 times**
two pair	**5 times**
three-flush with pair	**4 times**
three-straight with pair	**3 times**

Around 65 percent of the time your opponent will already have the better hand and there may very well be three more top bets to call before the showdown. Even when you still have the best hand you're less than a 2-to-1 favorite; but if your opponent has trips you're a 10- or 11-to-1 dog! That's the trap you want to avoid. Does it mean you should fold? The majority of times, yes, you should fold. But before you do, ask yourself a few quick questions to try to get a better read on his hand.

1. Were any 10s folded by the other players? If both of them were (a rare situation), then of course you should call rather than fold since he can't have trips.

2. If exactly one other 10 has been seen, did it appear right on 3rd Street, or later in the hand? If it was there at the beginning, it's less likely your opponent would have called a raise from a Jack while holding two 10s with a dead 10 in plain sight. In that case too, you ought to call.

3. If you saw one other 10, but it popped up on 4th or 5th Street, you're going to need more information. While it's true that your opponent needs the case 10 to have trips, still, try to recall how many spades came out during the hand. If spades are scarce, his chances of having started with a three-flush go up and once again, you're going to have to call.

4. If spades are all over the board, however, that starting pair of 10s looms more likely and you'd better fold against a typical player. Only against somebody who plays a "sloppy" wide range of hands would you call here.

5. Overall, in most cases no other 10s will have been seen at all, and that's when you should fold almost every time.

What about your own live cards? In this situation it's not all that important whether your other two Jacks are still live because, even if they were, at this point in the hand you'd only catch one of them about one time in 10. Your most realistic hope with this hand is to make Jacks up, which makes your 5s, 4s, and 9s much more important. If Jacks up doesn't figure to win, or it's going to be tough to make Jacks up, get out.

Finally, what if you can't remember whether any other 10s have been folded or how many spades were on the initial board and you have no idea how your opponent plays? In that case just fold your overpair when your opponent pairs his dreaded door card on 5th Street, unless you have made a four-flush or an open-end straight draw.

Now what about when somebody pairs his door card on 4th Street—or on 6th Street? When that happens on 4th Street, you might have to call four big bets to get to see his hand and the pot was smaller when it happened. Because of all that, pairing a door card on 4th Street should almost always end the hand. If it's you who have paired up, bet the maximum, unless you were the bring-in and didn't have to call a raise (which tells everybody you merely have two random cards in the hole). If an opponent pairs on the turn, just fold unless he was the bring-in with no raise on 3rd Street, or his other two 10s are out.

When an opponent pairs his door card on 6th Street, you're pretty close to the river and are getting better pot odds. Even if neither of his other pair cards came out, if your hand is live to make two pair, you can probably call on 6th Street. If you make Jacks up at the river, call if he bets. If you miss, review whether you saw many spades come out or straight cards surrounding his door card. If you don't see many, that's what he may have been on and again, you'd better call. But if his spades and straight cards are all over the place, he almost has to have two pair or trips, and you probably should give it up.

Concept #34: Sniffing Out Hidden Trips

Every once in a while, your opponent will make a big hand with absolutely no indication of it on board. Usually though, there will be telltale signs of this if you are paying attention. Suppose you are in the following heads-up Stud hand on 5th Street?

Your Hand

Opponent's Hand

You came into the pot raising with your buried 4s and this opponent just kept calling. Now when you bet again on 5th Street he raises you. Your hand looks as though it may very well be Kings up and his board just doesn't look like anything. That's the key! Why would he be raising here on an expensive street with a "nothing" board? If he's a responsible player, he'll usually have rolled up 6s or trip Jacks in this spot.

When a reasonable player turns aggressive out of nowhere later in the hand and you can't even put him on a draw, a light should start blinking in your head that says *trips! trips!*

True, there might a couple other hands he could have. But the pot usually won't be giving you a good enough price to call him down to the river and you should fold two small pair. Making these laydowns can save you serious money when you're beat, and you will be beaten most of those times.

Now what if you actually did have Kings up in this situation? It depends upon the sanity of your player. If he's a "no nonsense" sort and doesn't seem to be trying to play mind games with you, give it up. Only if he's wily enough to do something like this with buried Aces would you call.

Concept #35: The Critical 5th Street Crossroads

Fifth Street in 7 Stud is such a crossroads because that's the point at which the stakes double. Right there is where you must usually decide to either give it up now, or to go all the way. In a $50/$100 game you've probably paid $100 for your first five cards, but it might well cost another $300 to see the showdown.

Much has been written in poker books about what constitutes a playable starting hand on 3rd Street, but when you get to 5th Street, everything often changes. Those two 10s you started out with probably aren't worth a plugged nickel if an opponent now has open Jacks. In contrast, a lowly pair of 4s is actually a very playable hand against those Jacks if you now have something such as:

That's because with all those overcards you're nearly 50-50 to finish with Queens up, minimum. If you improve your 4s at all, it'll beat those Jacks even if he has or makes two pair, except for when your last two cards are something like 8/8. So it pays to know what hands are worth playing against what hands, and which ones should be mucked when you get to 5th Street.

Now, we all know that poker is a psychological game and determining where your opponent is at is paramount. But it doesn't do a lot of good to read your opponent's hand perfectly if you don't know the appropriate play for that situation. Many long-time successful players show disdain for poker percentages because their keen "street sense" has served them so well through the years. But times are changing. In the past, all the top players made their decisions with their instinctive noses. Although they had great poker instincts, many of their decisions still weren't optimal. That was okay, though, because none of their opponents did things any better.

Today, however, more and more state of the art analysis is being done on poker. Even though poker strategy is indeed psychological, those underlying percentages are at work whether you know them or not. If both you and your opponents have been making a certain play all these years that's a few percentage points less than optimum, you're going to begin losing ground when some new expert starts making the optimal play back at you in the same situation.

So then, what are the right plays to make with each hand on 5th Street? That depends upon many factors. Knowing what to do with your poker hand is not as simple as it is in casino blackjack. There, it's cut and dried because your blackjack opponent, the dealer, cannot adjust his play against you and your pot odds are pretty constant—generally even money. Hence, you know you should always hit with 16 against a dealer's 7 because your winning chances improve from 26 percent (by standing) to 30 percent (by hitting).

Below is a basic strategy chart for playing according to the odds on that all-important 5th Street in 7 Card Stud. In using it, however, you must make your best guess as to what you're up against. The better you can read what your opponent started out with, the more accurate your decisions will be at this critical juncture.

Be aware, however, that just as in blackjack, this basic chart does not take into account how many of yours or your opponents' cards may be live or dead. It assumes a full compliment of both helping and useless cards. Adjustments will sometimes be in order, but don't make the mistake of over-adjusting for this. For example, if you have:

when you think you're up against two smaller pair and you've seen one Queen, a 7, and a 3, your chances to improve are perfectly average if you've also seen 10 other non-helpers (23 percent of the remaining cards will still improve your hand, the same as with a full deck).

Also, the chart assumes a typical-sized pot on 5th Street. You should play a little tighter than the chart suggests if the pot was heads-up from the get-go with no earlier double raises, and play looser in an unusually large pot.

And, finally, this chart is aimed at heads-up 5th Street decisions. If the pot is multi-way, the other players' holdings can influence your correct play.

Keeping all those things in mind, here are the mathematically recommended decisions for most typical confrontations you'll encounter on 5th Street in 7 Stud.

5th Street 7 Stud Basic Strategy

You Have	You Read Your Opponent For	Right Play
1. 10-10-3-5-8	pair Jacks	**fold**
2. 10-10-3-5-8	9s up	**call**
3. 10-10-3-5-Q	pair Jacks	**call**

You Have	You Read Your Opponent For	Right Play
4. 10-10-3-5-Q	Jacks up	**fold**
5. 10-10-3-Q-K	Jacks up	**fold**
6. 4-4-A-K-Q	Jacks up	**call**
7. 10-10-5-5-8	pair Jacks	**call/raise**
8. 10-10-5-5-8	Jacks up	**fold**
9. 10-10 with four-flush	pair Jacks	**raise**
10. 10-10 with four-flush	Jacks up	**call**
11. 10-10 with four-flush	trip Jacks	**????**

With **hand #1**, you have an underpair and no over-cards. Your winning chances here are too slim, since even when you make a second pair your opponent will often do the same.

Hand #2 is a clear-cut call assuming your opponent started with a split pair and has now made something like 9-6-6 on board. If the hand was played in such a way, however, that you're pretty sure you're up against a bigger buried pair, you'd be too heavy an underdog to call.

With **hand #3**, your overcard Queen is enough to make calling to the river worthwhile against two Jacks, unless something ominous develops on 6th Street. Again, though, be alert that you're not actually up against buried Kings or Aces.

Hand #4 should be thrown away since most of your improvements will still only give you 10s up, a loser.

Hand #5 is a pretty close decision that usually favors folding by a small margin. If both overcards are totally live, however, you can call to the river.

Hand #6: With three moderately live overcards to your opponent's two pair, you've easily got enough to go all the way.

Hand #7: On average, two small pair on 5th Street are just a tiny favorite over one obvious bigger pair who could have a hidden two pair by chance. There's so little to be gained by raising here that you might want to hold back until 6th Street to see if your opponent improves in sight there.

Hand #8: Two small pair are a huge underdog against two bigger pair on 5th Street. You'll fill up only one time in six and occasionally still lose to his bigger full house.

Hand #9: One smaller pair with a flush draw is actually a small overall favorite over one overpair who might possibly have two pair, but probably doesn't. Raising is usually correct since that may induce the Jacks to check on the next card. If you've improved, keep right on betting. If you've missed, go for a check.

Hand #10: If your opponent already has two pair, the flush is your only plausible out. Hence, you can only call, but folding would generally be wrong.

Hand #11 is a close one. Here's where live cards, the size of the pot, and the confidence of your read can easily swing things either way. First and foremost, if you could be certain you were against trips you should definitely fold since one-third of your flushes will lose to your opponent's eventual full house. But if it's just a generic "paired door card" situation and your flush draw is pretty live, lean towards calling. If you had Queens (an overpair) with your four-flush rather than 10s, calling would be almost automatic because of the few extra times you'd win just by making trips.

Concept #36: Playing Heads Up

Strategically speaking, 7 Stud should usually be a heads-up game because the lead hand is generally best off isolating itself against one inferior hand. If it looks like your hand is the one that's in the lead, you should try to do what's necessary to get the pot heads-up unless you have a nearly invincible powerhouse. That typically means:

1. Betting when you have the high board and nobody is likely to bet if you check.
2. Check/raising if it looks like the player on your right will bet when you check. (You can then make it two cold bets to the rest of the field, driving players out).
3. Raising when you're not high after the high board bets.

If you probably don't have the best hand, but it's a playable one, you usually want to get in as cheaply as possible. When you're in that kind of situation, you want to be careful that you don't get squeezed into calling extra bets in order to play. Here's an example:

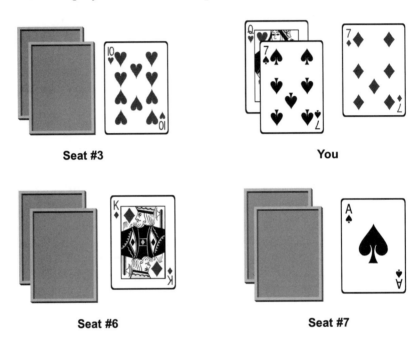

Seat #3   You

Seat #6   Seat #7

After the low card brings it in, the 10 raises it and you're next. Even though you have an overcard to the raiser's door card, there are two real overcards still to act behind you. One of them may re-raise and you just can't fade the action in that kind of predicament, so muck your pair right now! If there was only one threatening overcard behind you, you could probably go ahead and call.

Now, just to show you what a complex game 7 Stud is, if your Q-7/7 was 7-7/Q and those two cards behind you weren't overcards, you'd probably want to re-raise the 10 if you felt you were the better player. You're going to play anyway, but now there are three extra reasons to re-raise:

1. Re-raising represents that you have a pair of Queens and your opponent may very well give up his hand by 5th Street if he doesn't improve.
2. Your re-raise may get you a free card on a later street if you need it.
3. You have the outside bonus of getting all kinds of action should you hit a harmless looking 7.

When you have the overcard kicker as your door card rather than in the hole, your statistical chance to make the best hand is exactly the same. But your chance to win the pot without making the best hand goes up. It's fairly important with this play, however, that you feel confident in trying to muscle your opponent. If he knows he can outplay you, he's more likely to stick with you card-by-card, try to figure out what you're up to, and not give you what you want when you want it. Know your players!

Concept #37: Playing Multi-Way

Sometimes when you have a decent hand, your only choice is to either come into a multi-way pot or throw your hand away. In general, winning a multi-way pot takes a better hand than if the play were heads-up. That's because of all the extra hands drawing against you. So then, do you need a better starting hand to play in a multi-way pot? Well, sort of.

More specifically, a different variation of hands tends to do better against several opponents. You see, in heads-up play, big starting pairs are your bread and butter hands. You'd love to have two Queens against a smaller pair in a heads-up pot. But in a four-way pot, while two Queens are usually still playable, you'd probably rather have an Ace high three-flush. By the time you get to 5th Street, if the three-flush now has a four-flush and the pair of Queens hasn't improved, the four-flush has a much better chance to win a multi-way pot than the Queens.

Don't misunderstand, it's not that the four-flush is a favorite over the Queens because it's not. When there's multi-way action though, the Queens have to outrun the four-flush, plus the other hands chasing it. But if the four-flush makes his flush, he probably won't have any trouble beating everybody.

For this reason, holdings with bigger hand potential, even though they may be nothing at the moment, play better than high pairs or a small pair with a big kicker when the pot is multi-way. This is even true to the extent that if the pot is at least four-way on 4th Street and there's a bet but no raise, you should probably take another card off with the likes of:

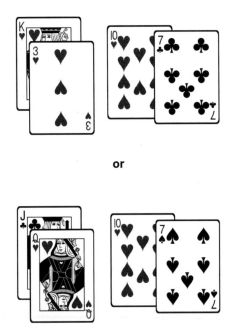

or

where hands like these should often be thrown away if you find yourself heads-up. But when you are getting better pot odds, you can try to catch a heart to the three-flush and a King or a 9 to the big three-straight. In both cases there are eight to ten cards that will give you a draw to a big hand. If you don't snag what you're looking for (a four-flush or an open-ender), you are done with it at 5th Street. The stuff you generally want to get rid of when the pot is still four-way on 4th Street are hands like:

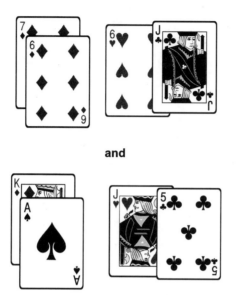

and

These would need to improve way too much on the next card to give you enough to go up against several opponents. About all you could really use with the two 6s would be another 6, or possibly a Jack. With the A/K/J/5, the only really big help would be to pair your door card. With either hand, you have just a few helping cards, and then you might be in trouble.

Concept #38: Do You Want the Third Hand In or Out?

Concepts #36 and #37 bring up a curious strategy dilemma that arises regularly in 7 Stud. Since the best hand generally does best playing heads up, does a playable second best hand want a third player in there or not? Take a look at the following scenario:

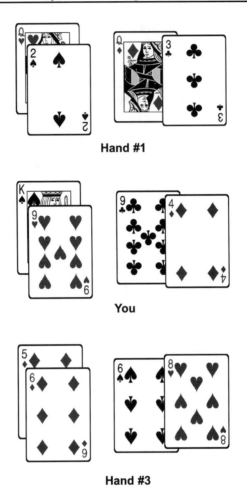

Hand #1

You

Hand #3

If you have the pair of 9s, your King kicker makes your hand worthwhile playing against probable Queens. But what about hand #3? Do your 9s do better overall if the two 6s played, or if he were out? And if you have the chance to drive the 6s out with a raise, should you do it? Your first question might be, "How do I know he has a pair of 6s? Maybe he's got buried deuces, or even 10s, or a busted three-flush, or a straight draw." Yes, he could have any of these. And if he has one of his better holdings you'd love to knock him out, but then he's probably not going anywhere, even with a raise! Yet, if he has one of the weaker hands, you actually do better with his money and his hand in the pot! For this reason: *It's generally not worth raising to get the third hand out when you are running second in a three-way pot.*

The one who usually gets hurt the worst by having a third player in the pot is the lead hand. But if you're already second best, and your hand is playable, usually just call to see what develops. In most cases where you do raise to get it heads-up having the second best hand, your chief benefit comes not specifically from being heads-up, but from effectively representing a stronger hand than you actually have (see the "7-7/Q" example mentioned in the second to last paragraph of Concept #36).

Okay, now what if it looks like you are the one running third in a three-way pot? If you've got the busted three-flush it's a no-brainer, get out of anything less than a four-way pot. But if you have a playable hand like that pair of 6s with the two-suited 5-6-8 shown on the previous page, you'd greatly improve your chances to win if you could blow out an apparent pair of 9s with a raise. Then you'd immediately improve from third best to second best. That, however, would require you to be next to act after the Queen bets. If your table position is such that you can make it two cold bets to the 9 and it seems he might give up his hand under pressure, go ahead and raise. This would be another one of those fairly rare times when it's worth raising without having the best hand.

For more on raising to get heads up, see Concepts #17 and #23. Notice at the end of Concept #17 that you have an underpair (two 6s) to several higher door cards with two overcards of your own (a King and Queen) in a four-way pot. Four-way pots are a little different than three-way when you're running second. If you're a pretty close second, such as in this case, you're almost a co-leader and should try to trim the field with a check/raise.

In contrast, with Concept #23 you already have an overpair against a probable smaller two pair, plus another opponent who has an undercard door card. In this case, every improvement will give you Kings up or better, a strong hand against that field. Now you do better by leaving the third opponent in since he poses very little danger to you whenever you improve, and you must improve or you lose anyway.

Concept #39: Betting at the River

The hand isn't over as soon as you reach 7th Street. There's still money to be made or saved at the river. Good Stud players know how to gain extra value on the end with a winner and save bets when they're in trouble. The following example illustrates one of the most common situations you'll ever find yourself in on 7th Street—I've been there plenty!

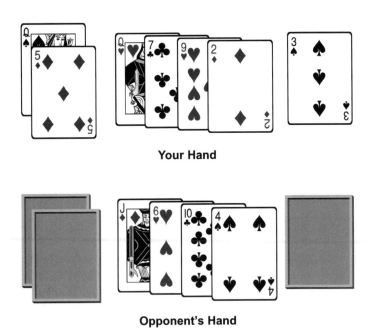

Your Hand

Opponent's Hand

You failed to improve your two Queens at the river and you think your opponent was probably calling all the way with a pair of Jacks. If he missed at the river also, he may not call if you bet—but if he made Jacks up, he'll definitely call and you'll lose that river bet. Yet, if you check, he'll probably go ahead and bet if he made two pair and you may feel obliged to call, keeping him honest. What to do?

Here's where each individual situation depends upon the tendencies of your opponent. First, ask yourself if this player would call your bet at the river with only two Jacks. Also, what are the chances that he'll bet if you check—and if he does bet, how many of those times will he have two pair (or better) and how many times might he take it into his head to bluff? Here's how to put all that together in reaching an effective decision.

1. If you think he'll call with just a pair of Jacks and he showed no aggression on 5th or 6th Street (by raising)—bet right out, since he probably still had one pair heading to the river and will fail to improve there about seven times out of ten.

2. If you think he's more likely to fold with one pair when you bet—check, since you won't get called unless he's improved and you're beaten.

> **a.** If he bets after you check, fold against somebody who will bet only when he's improved, but call if he's the type who might bet because you showed weakness.

> **b.** However, if he's a tight, careful player who might fold two pair when he's been check/raised, then try that, but only occasionally.

Now what happens when the two hands are reversed; you have the pair of Jacks against probable Queens and your opponent bets at the river?

1. If you didn't improve and are nearly sure he had the bigger pair all the way—fold.

2. If you missed, but there's reasonable doubt about his having an overpair—call.

3. If you made two pair you must nearly always call—unless you're positive he'd never bet one overpair on the end for value, and virtually never bluffs.

How about when your opponent checks with those apparent Queens?

1. If you missed, in the vast majority of cases you must check along.

2. If you've made two pair—bet.
    a. If he check/raises after you bet—fold, since it's such a rare occurrence that a player will check-raise on the end as a bluff.

As you can see, managing your hand on the river skillfully with your one pair/two pair hands is a tricky task with several variables. Many other 7th Street situations will also arise, but the bulk of those can be played a tad more systematically.

When you have two big pair or trips against an apparent flush draw, for example, you should usually check because you probably won't get called unless your opponent makes his flush and beats you.

Conversely, when you have a made flush or straight against apparent trips, you can normally bet it at the river because your opponent is likely to call with his trips and will make a full house only about two times out of nine. So even if you pay off his raise the two times he fills up, losing four bets total, you still collect seven bets the times he calls you with trips.

Chapter 6

Texas Hold'em

Texas Hold'em has probably become the most-played poker game in public card rooms. There are a couple of good reasons for it. First, Hold'em is fast. If you're running a poker room, your dealer can get out about 40 hands of Hold'em per hour compared to maybe 30 hands of 7 Stud—and even fewer hands in high/low split games. Since most poker games are raked "x" dollars per pot, Hold'em is generally more profitable for the house.

There's still another reason why Texas Hold'em has become so popular. It's because Hold'em is simpler to figure out. With only two hole cards of your own and five community cards on the table, the number of opponents' hand possibilities is cut way down as compared to Stud poker. For example, if at the end of the hand, the final board looks like this:

you know for sure the best hand anybody could possibly have is a set of trips. In fact, an Ace/Queen in the pocket, making a pair of Queens with an Ace kicker, would be a big favorite to take down the money in this spot. "Top pair" against a "dead" board is actually a pretty big hand in Hold'em. On the other hand if the board read:

and you have that same Ace/Queen with no clubs, even though you have three Queens this time, they're almost certainly no good since anybody with one club, an 8, a King or pocket 9s, 10s, or Jacks has you beaten. Similar principles apply on the flop, which can strongly indicate whether your hand is worth pursuing further. For reasons like these, it's easier to tell where you are at in a Hold'em hand. That tends to draw players who are new to casino poker towards the Hold'em table.

Now, I'm not suggesting that you can play limit Hold'em totally by rote, the way a basic strategy player plays blackjack. In any form of poker you can't unequivocally say, "Always do this," or, "Never do that." It always depends upon what your opponents may have taken into their own heads to do. This psychological element is what makes poker the intense mental challenge it is.

Still, Hold'em's variables are less complex than other poker games, hence a more concise and preconceived strategy can be developed for it. So winning limit Hold'em can indeed be played a bit more "by the book," particularly before the flop.

Concept #40: Hold'em's 169 Two-Card Starting Hands

The first step in recognizing Hold'em's simplicity comes when you consider your starting hands. In 7 Card Stud you can be dealt any one of 1,495 strategically different starting hands, counting buried pairs, split pairs, roll-ups, three-flushes, etc. But in Hold'em, 169 sets of possible hole cards is all you'll ever see. That makes things a lot more concise. As with any form of poker, winning at Hold'em begins with playing the right starting hands. Some Hold'em hands are so much better than others, it's a joke. To give you an idea of what I mean, a pocket pair of Aces will beat an unsuited 7/2 seven times out of eight after all the cards are out! Those same two Aces will beat a 7/10 five times out of six. The point is, most of those 169 hands should never be played—*unless* you're one of the blinds and don't have to put any additional money into the pot. Paying to see the flop with substandard cards has a way of snowballing into costly mistakes later in the hand. That's why you need to build your game upon a solid foundation.

There are basically four different categories of starting hands. They are *unsuited hands, suited hands, connectors,* and *pairs.* All 169 hands are listed by category on the next page. Take a look at them and get a feel for just how many different holdings you and/or your opponents can have—because this is all there is:

Unsuited		Suited		Connectors	Pairs
A/Q	J/5	*A/Q*	J/5	*A/K suited*	*A/A*
A/J	J/4	*A/J*	J/4	*A/K*	*K/K*
A/10	J/3	*A/10*	J/3	*K/Q suited*	*Q/Q*
A/9	J/2	*A/9*	J/2	*K/Q*	*J/J*
A/8	10/8	*A/8*	*10/8*	*Q/J suited*	*10/10*
A/7	10/7	A/7	10/7	*Q/J*	*9/9*
A/6	10/6	A/6	10/6	*J/10 suited*	*8/8*
A/5	10/5	A/5	10/5	*J/10*	*7/7*
A/4	10/4	A/4	10/4	*10/9 suited*	*6/6*
A/3	10/3	A/3	10/3	*10/9*	*5/5*
K/J	10/2	*K/J*	10/2	*9/8 suited*	*4/4*
K/10	9/7	*K/10*	9/7	*9/8*	*3/3*
K/9	9/6	*K/9*	9/6	*8/7 suited*	*2/2*
K/8	9/5	K/8	9/5	8/7	
K/7	9/4	K/7	9/4	*7/6 suited*	
K/6	9/3	K/6	9/3	7/6	
K/5	9/2	K/5	9/2	*6/5 suited*	
K/4	8/6	K/4	8/6	6/5	
K/3	8/5	K/3	8/5	5/4 suited	
K/2	8/4	K/2	8/4	5/4	
Q/10	8/3	*Q/10*	8/3	4/3 suited	
Q/9	8/2	*Q/9*	8/2	4/3	
Q/8	7/5	Q/8	7/5	3/2 suited	
Q/7	7/4	Q/7	7/4	3/2	
Q/6	7/3	Q/6	7/3	A/2 suited	
Q/5	7/2	Q/5	7/2	A/2	
Q/4	6/4	Q/4	6/4		
Q/3	6/3	Q/3	6/3		
Q/2	6/2	Q/2	6/2		
J/9	5/3	*J/9*	5/3		
J/8	5/2	J/8	5/2		
J/7	4/2	J/7	4/2		
J/6		J/6			

Concept #41: Hold'em Is Basically a High Card Game

Back in Concept #31 it was stressed how important it is to play live cards in 7 Card Stud. But in Hold'em, there are no exposed cards to eliminate. Your upcards are your opponents' upcards. While Stud is a "live card" game, it turns out that Hold'em is basically a "high card" game. On the whole, you just can't beat this game playing low or medium cards.

From Concept #40, you get an entire picture of everything that you or your opponents can be dealt before the flop. It's really not all that complicated. If you're playing something like 9/6 when your opponents have high cards and everybody misses the flop, you are beat. If everybody flops a pair, you're beat again. The only time you win is when you hit and they miss. Those are bad odds. Why not play high cards and have it the other way around?

Successful Hold'em players say that to win, you must play very strong starters most of the time, but know when to sneak in there with a mediocre start. That's basically true, but don't get carried away. You'll see overimaginative people reraising before the flop with an absolute piece o' cheese like 8/5 and occasionally taking down a huge pot. That might work for a while, but six months later those guys are generally back at poker boot camp.

Look at the chart back in Concept #40. Fifty of the best hands there are in this game have been singled out. You'll find them in **_enlarged bold and italics_**. You can build your game around these 50 starters, leaving everything else out—for the most part.

Some of these 50 hands you'll virtually always play and others you'll play only when things are right for it; that's the trick. Let's pick them out right now.

1. Take unsuited Aces down through **A/9**, unsuited Kings through **K/9**, unsuited Queens through **Q/9**, and a **J/9**.

2. Take suited Aces down through **A/7**, suited Kings through **K/9**, suited Queens through **Q/9**, a suited **J/9**, and a suited **10/8**.
3. Take unsuited connectors down through **10/9** and suited connectors down through **6/5**.
4. Take **any Pair**.

Try to get these 50 hands filed away in your head; you pretty much want to steer away from everything else, *except under unusual circumstances*.

Now, when and how should you play these 50 hands? That depends upon many things, the most important of which is:

Concept #42: Your Position

Your table position means far more in "flop-style" poker than in Stud, because your position will remain the same through all four betting rounds. If you're first to act, you stay first; if you're last, you stay last until the hand is over. I don't have to tell you there's an edge in knowing who has called, raised and folded before it comes your turn to act. For that reason, you should raise with a minimally playable hand like

if you are dead last against only the blinds, but you should fold if you act first right after the blinds. Why? Picture yourself in the #3 seat (under the gun) in a $30/$60 game. The small blind must put in $15 and the big blind posts his mandatory $30. The hole cards are dealt and you are next with six or seven players yet to act behind you. Looking down, you find that Q/10 unsuited. It's $30 to call, $60 to raise. Now an unsuited Q/10 is maybe about the 40th best hand you can be dealt out of 169. It's likely to have the two blinds beaten, but what about all those players behind you? The odds say that a couple of players are holding better stuff than that and you'll hear from them when it gets raised to $60. If you play that hand without seeing most of the players throw their hands away first, you'll be taking the worst of it. Get out.

Now let's reverse it and put you in the ninth seat of a nine-handed game, known as being the button. Six players fold after the blinds and now it's your turn. This time there are only two people who can have a hand better than yours—the two blinds. Now you're the favorite with that Q/10, so you should raise. Besides being a probable favorite, if anybody calls your raise you'll have position on him because you will get to act last throughout the hand.

What if somebody in the middle raises when you have that Q/10 way back in the ninth seat? Fundamentally, you should fold since he probably wouldn't have raised from that position without something stronger than just a Q/10. There are other considerations, however, so just before you throw your hand away, ask yourself the following questions.

How tight or loose is the raiser? How passive or aggressive is he? How tough is he to play against after the flop? Since you've got position on him, if he's loose and aggressive (which means he doesn't need that good a hand to raise), you might give him a call. See what the flop brings and take it from there. All things being equal though, you should generally fold a marginal hand like Q/10 unsuited whenever somebody puts money into the pot in front of you.

Finally, what if there's a raise and a call in front of you when you have Q/10? Simple: you don't belong in the hand, so muck it!

The preceding example was intended to give you a general idea how much position affects your strategy in Hold'em. Now, let's get on to defining in practical terms, when and how to play those 50 hands before the flop.

Concept #43: Early Position

Your position at the Hold'em table should be thought of in three separate categories; early, middle, and late. In a full nine- or ten-handed game, early position would essentially be the first two seats after the blinds (seats 3 and 4). Middle position would be the next three seats (seats 5, 6, and 7), and late position would be the last two or three seats to act.

Up front is where you need your best hole cards because of your lack of information on who is about to do what. You won't play anywhere near 50 hands from up here, and most of the hands you will play should normally be brought in with a raise.

When You're the First One In

When you're first to act, or the #3 seat has folded and you're in the #4 hole, you should come in raising with:

unsuited high hands of A/Q and A/J
suited high hands of A/Q and A/J
unsuited connector of A/K
suited connectors of A/K and K/Q
pair of 9s or higher.

but just call with:

suited high hands of A/10 and K/J
suited connector of Q/J
pair of 8s.

These 17 premium hands are about all that you'll be willing to kick off the action with. If you have anything less, be very inclined to fold from this disadvantageous position.

When There's a Caller

What if you're in the #4 seat and the #3 seat has just called? Raise with the 12 stronger hands of the original 17, but just call along with these remaining five weaker hands:

**A/J unsuited
A/10 suited, K/J suited and Q/J suited
pair of 8s**

However, now you'll also want to call with hands like:

**J/10 suited
pair of 7s or 6s.**

The reason? These three hands may not be as good as the first caller's, but two flat calls up front tend to encourage multi-way action and that would be a good spot to flop a flush draw, a straight draw, or a set of trips.

When There's Been a Raise

Now instead of just calling, what if the #3 seat has raised in front of you? Then re-raise with:

**unsuited connector of A/K
suited connector of A/K
pair of 10s or higher**

but just call with:

**unsuited high hand of A/Q
suited high hand of A/Q
suited connector of K/Q
pair of 9s**

and fold everything else.

That should be the general flavor of your play from up front. Now, bear in mind that after all these specifics, it still remains true that nothing in poker should be etched in stone. There can always be reasons why you should manage your hand differently this particular time around. If the #3 seat raised in front of you, for example, and the game is loose, you'd probably also want to call (rather than fold) with something like an A/J suited or Q/J suited because you're likely to see multi-way action. Just be sure, if you're going to deviate from the basics, that you've got a sound reason and it's not simply because you feel like playing. The poker gods are extremely unforgiving of undisciplined poker players.

Concept #44: Middle Position

In the fifth through seventh seats you have a lot to think about. Chances are you are not in there alone with the blinds. If you are alone, you can play somewhat looser than up front since there are fewer people behind you who can have a better hand than yours.

When You're the First One In

When in this optimal situation, you should come in raising with:

unsuited high hands of A/Q and A/J
suited high hands of A/Q, A/J, A/10 and K/J
unsuited connectors of A/K and K/Q
suited connectors of A/K, K/Q, and Q/J
pair of 8s or higher

but just come in calling with:

suited high hands of K/10 and Q/10
unsuited connector of Q/J
suited connectors of J/10 and 10/9
pair of 7s or 6s.

That is basically 25 hands you'll look for to start off the action from this position. If somebody else has already come in, however, you have to be more careful.

When There Is a Caller(s)

If they've merely called in front of you, then raise with:

unsuited high hand of A/Q
suited high hands of A/Q and A/J
unsuited connectors of A/K and K/Q
suited connectors of A/K and K/Q
pair of 8s or higher

and just call along with:

> **unsuited high hand of A/J**
> **suited high hands of A/10, K/J, K/10 and Q/10**
> **unsuited connectors of Q/J and J/10**
> **suited connectors of Q/J, J/10 and 10/9**
> **as well as a pair of 5s through 7s**

but fold the likes of:

> **unsuited A/10 and K/J.**

When There's Been a Raise

Now what if there's been a raise in front of you? In that case, you can re-raise only with:

> **suited high hand of A/Q**
> **unsuited connector of A/K**
> **suited connector of A/K**
> **pair of 10s or higher**

and call with:

> **suited high hand of A/J**
> **unsuited high hand of A/Q**
> **suited connectors of K/Q and Q/J**
> **pair of 9s**

then fold everything else.

Concept #45: Late Position

From the #8 seat or later, your game can open up considerably, particularly if there's little or no action in front of you. In the classic but fairly rare situation where it's just you and the blinds, you should actually break form and raise with about the top 50 percent of all 169 hands, folding only the bottom half.

When You're the First One In

Virtually always raise with any hand you're going to play here as an extra inducement to push out either or both blinds. Your approximate raising hands are:

> **any Ace or King hand**
> **any Queen or Jack with at least a 7 kicker**
> **any connectors down through 6/5, plus a 10/8**
> **any pair**

and just let the blinds have the pot if you've got less than that. If you're not alone with the blinds, however, you're going to have to play it quite a bit more honest.

When There Is a Caller(s)

If there are only callers in front of you but no raise, then go ahead and raise with:

> **unsuited high hands of A/Q and A/J**
> **suited high hands of A/Q, A/J and K/J**
> **unsuited connectors of A/K and K/Q**
> **suited connectors of A/K, K/Q and Q/J**
> **pair of 10s or higher**

and just call with:

> **unsuited high hands of A/10, A/9, K/J, K/10, K/9, Q/10, Q9 and J/9**
> **suited high hands of A/10, A/9, A/8, K/10, K/9, Q/10, Q/9, J/9 and 10/8**
> **unsuited connectors of Q/J, J/10, 10/9 and 9/8**
> **suited connectors of J/10, 10/9, 9/8, 8/7, 7/6, and 6/5**
> **pair of deuces through 9s.**

This is where you'll generally be willing to put all 50 of your basic hands into play. If there's been a raise in front of you, though, a lot of your non-premium hands won't be worth taking a shot with.

When There's Been a Raise

When it's already two bets to come in, re-raise it with:

no unsuited non-connectors
suited high hands of A/Q
unsuited connectors of A/K
suited connectors of A/K, K/Q
pair of 10s or higher

and just call with:

unsuited high hands of A/Q
suited high hands of A/J, K/J
unsuited connector of K/Q
suited connectors of Q/J
pair of 7s, 8s or 9s.

Again, I'll stress that poker, Hold'em included, is not a game to be played by rote. Every one of the previous concepts contains a "fudge factor." Understand that if there were three middle or late callers with no raise, that's a much more inviting situation than if there was a raise right up front and no callers when it gets to you. In the first scenario, you should loosen up quite a bit because nobody thought enough of their hands to raise and you can now get some pretty good odds on your drawing hands such as 9/8 unsuited or 6/5 suited. In the second scenario you should tighten up even more than that list suggests because you're probably up against a pretty strong hand and aren't getting good pot odds. Now, you might want to just call, rather than raise, with an A/Q suited and fold, rather than call, with hands like K/J suited or Q/J suited. These adjustments ought to be tweaked still further based upon which types of players did what. There is no substitute for knowing your players and reading the situation. That's where winning poker becomes more of an art than a science.

Concept #46: Playing Out of the Blinds

BIG BLIND: If you're the big blind in a $20/$40 Hold'em game, you've got $20 in the pot before you even see your cards. The action begins on your immediate left and if nobody's raised by the time it comes back around to you, you are in automatically. Your blind is live, however, which means you do have the opportunity to raise just like everybody else. This is the moment when you'll either rap on the table, signifying for the dealer to go ahead and deal the flop, or you'll put in another $20 and raise it to $40.

If you raise, the action goes around the table one more time and everybody must either call, re-raise or fold. Now, understand that anybody who has already called the first bet will most likely call your raise. So if you decide to raise from the big blind position, you should be doing it because you want to build the pot rather than be trying to drive players out. For that reason, and because you'll be playing the hand out of position, you should raise only with a super hand when you're the big blind—such as:

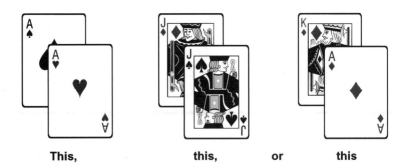

This,   **this,**   **or**   **this**

As always, there are exceptions. A classic one might be when you find yourself alone with the small blind and you don't want him to play. If he's the type who might throw his hand away for another $20 after having already voluntarily put in $10, you probably should raise with your baby pairs such as 2/2 or 5/5. And if you've got a healthier pocket pair such as 8/8 or 9/9, you definitely want to put the pressure on him.

Another exception (and this is debatable) might be that with pocket Aces, maybe you ought to just rap on the table and then bet the flop as though you've caught a piece of it. Anyone who flopped top pair will probably raise you and you can now build the pot while driving other players out.

SMALL BLIND: If you're the small blind in that same $20/$40 game, when it comes around to you it'll cost $10 to play if there was no raise and $30 if there was. Since you'll be first to act throughout the entire hand, you still want to play pretty selectively here even though you'll already be halfway in (so to speak) when it hasn't been raised. The types of hands you'll call that last half bet with would be holdings that can make something big, such as:

any medium or small pair
unsuited connectors of 8/7 or higher
suited connectors of 5/4 or higher
any "one-gap" connectors of J/9 or higher.

With bigger pocket pairs such as 10s or higher, just come right in with a raise. Part of the reason for that is to remove the big blind from the hand.

In addition, a few Hold'em stakes are structured with the small blind being two-thirds of the big blind. In $15/$30 Hold'em for example, the blinds are $10 and $15. At $75/$150, they're $50 and $75. When this is the case and there's been no raise, you can limp in and see the flop with a veritable multitude of hands, as long as the big blind isn't a notorious raiser. Your calling hands here can include holdings as weak as 10/7 offsuit, 8/6 offsuit and 6/4 suited. However, I think you should still stay away from the "one high card/one low card" hands such as K/5 offsuit.

Since the majority of Hold'em pots are raised before the flop, you won't be able to limp in for half a bet all that often. When it's 1.5 bets to you, there are simply very few hands you can play out of position like this. Here you'd be pretty much limited to:

**pair of 9s or higher
unsuited A/Q
any A/K
suited K/Q or Q/J.**

Concept #47: Hold'em Is Not a Draw Out Game

Once the flop comes down in Hold'em, the lead hand holds up and wins the pot more often than in any other form of casino poker. It's important to realize this if you're going to be a Hold'em player. Here's a common example:

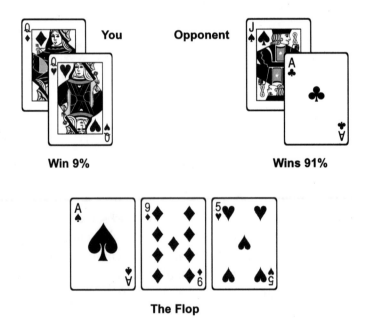

You   **Opponent**

Win 9%   **Wins 91%**

The Flop

The percentage figures beneath each hand show their respective chances to win the pot if they both played all the way. You had a great hand before the flop, but when that Ace fell you became a 10-to-1 underdog. You need to hit a Queen to win. That gives you only two "outs" in the deck, the two remaining Queens. Here's another illustration:

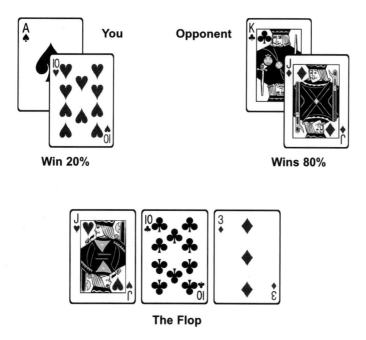

Win 20%   **Wins 80%**

The Flop

This time your second best pair is only a 4-to-1 underdog. The reason is that besides having two live 10s to hit, three other Aces would make you Aces up, giving you five basic outs (unless your opponent happened to hold A/J rather than K/J). So when you flop the second best pair in Hold'em, you're usually anywhere from a 4-to-1 to a 10-to-1 underdog to win. That's a lot worse than in 7 Card Stud where a starting pair of Jacks with no overcard is only about a 2-to-1 dog to a pair of Queens. In Omaha poker for that matter, you will often flop the nut straight and still be the underdog! Let's do one last Hold'em example:

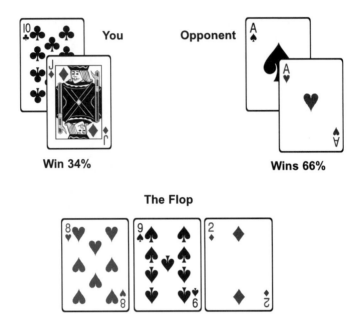

You   **Opponent**

Win 34%   **Wins 66%**

The Flop

Here, you're only about a 2-to-1 dog to win the money because any one of four 7s or four Queens will make you a straight. If the flop was 7/9/2, giving you a "gut shot" (inside straight draw) you'd be a 4-to-1 underdog.

These examples were given to illustrate that when you don't have the best hand on the flop in Hold'em, you're pretty far behind—unless you have a four-flush or an open-end straight draw. This is one of the reasons why Hold'em strategy is a bit more cut and dried than probably all other casino poker games. In most cases, if you can determine that you are behind on the flop, you should give it up. As always, however, there are exceptions, and these exceptions come up frequently enough that they need to be discussed. But first, let's look at your most desirable objective.

Concept #48: Flopping Top Pair

Your bread and butter hand in Hold'em is when you flop top pair as in the following example:

Your Hand

The Flop

On average, one big pair wins the pot in this game. Flopping top pair is a textbook outcome for you; just play the two high cards like the book says and have one of them be the highest card in the flop. On days when this keeps on happening, life is usually pretty good.

But there are different grades of top pair. The example above is a desirable one, but not perfect. It's desirable because the other two cards are spread out and unsuited—therefore it's unlikely that anybody will end up making a straight or flush. Yet it's still an insecure hand because an Ace can come on a later street and wreck you. So now let's look at two more flops, in both you hit the top pair—but one better and one worse than the example just shown above:

Your Hand

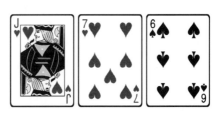

The Flop

You do have top pair here, but it's in considerable jeopardy. First, somebody else may also have a Jack, but with a better kicker. Next, if an Ace, King, or Queen comes on either of the last two cards, you might easily be beaten. And, finally, any heart, 5 or 8 might give somebody a straight or a flush.

When you flop a top pair as vulnerable as this one and the pot is multi-way, if you're in an early seat it may be best to just check since you'll probably get raised anyway. After you check, somebody will almost certainly bet a versatile flop like this, then you should call. If 4th Street turns out to be a nonthreatening card (no Ace, King, Queen, or heart), then you can bet the larger 4th Street amount which will drive out nearly anything but a flush draw or open-end straight draw. Then at the river you should probably revert to checking again since most hands that could call there will have you beat—plus, your check just might induce a busted draw to bluff.

If you're heads-up with one opponent, however, your betting strategy should be quite different. If you're first to act, or if it's been checked to you, bet, since there aren't so many chances for every dangerous hand to be out there. If it's a bet in front of you, raise—your opponent is out of position and will have to decide how to handle you on 4th Street. If a scare card comes on the turn and your opponent bets, your judgment will have to be your guide. If he checks, you should probably bet again—and there are many hands he could have that he'll fold for this bigger bet.

Flopping top pair when three overcards, a flush card, or a straight card can beat you is not a warm and fuzzy position to be in. In this spot you should be thinking more about the possibility of having to give up than how to maximize profits. Now let's take a look at a more comfortable top pair situation:

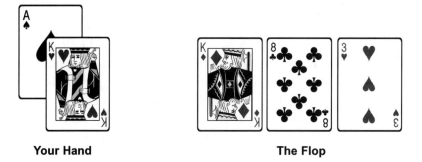

Your Hand   **The Flop**

This time, there's no straight draw or flush draw on the board. Also, you've got an Ace kicker and might make some money from another player who also paired his King. And finally if an Ace comes later, your Aces and Kings might earn extra profit from somebody who played an Ace. Your hand is really rather secure. If you have only a couple of opponents and are first, you might want to check. If there's a bet, check/raise. If there's not, bet out on 4th Street. Your opponents will be less likely to believe you have a King at that point. In this premium top pair situation, you can afford to get a little fancy and try to earn an extra bet or two.

Concept #49: Flopping Second Pair

Let's face it. Many times you'll flop a pair in Hold'em, but it won't be top pair. When you've got those pocket Queens shown back in Concept #47 and an Ace flops followed by significant betting (classically if there's been a bet and a call), you've simply got to fold. Somebody will usually have an Ace and you just can't put any money into the pot being a 10-to-1 underdog. A delicate exception might be if the pot was heads up and you judge that there's a reasonable chance your opponent would bet without having an Ace in his hand.

Now what about when you have that A/10 hand and the J/10/3 flops, again giving you second pair (also shown in

Concept #47)? This time, with five outs to make two pair or trips your hand is still a decided underdog, but not hopeless. If it looks like you can get in for just one bet on the flop (and that's an all-important "if"), your standard strategy would be to call and see the turn card (4th Street). Your pot odds will usually support calling one small bet, but not a bet and a raise (if the pot is unusually small, fold for even one bet). If you miss on the turn, however, fold, since the size of the bet doubles on the next card and your five-outer will cost too much to pursue compared to what you could win. Now suppose you've come into the pot with:

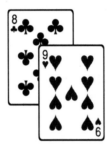

and the flop comes down:

This time you've flopped third pair. What now? If hitting your kicker, thereby making 9s and 8s, doesn't seem likely to make anybody a straight, then again you can call to see the turn card if there's been only a bet and you're almost certain it won't get raised behind you. You'd be very wary of continuing past the flop with your 8/9 however if the board was something like:

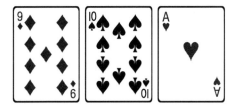

Now, making two pair here might just cost you more money because the board will now contain a three-straight. So be careful when you decide to call a bet on the flop with what you think is *five outs*. Sometimes hitting your kicker will make somebody else an even better hand and you'll find out you really had only *two outs*! Unless it looks as if your kicker is a card that nobody else could use, just fold your second and third pairs on the flop if there's a bet.

Concept #50: Flopping a Primary Draw

There are two basic types of primary draws you can hit on the flop. The first is an open-end straight draw as illustrated with your J/10 and the flop of 8/9/2 shown at the end of Concept #47. There, you'll eventually make your straight just about one-third of the time. A second, and even more desirable draw, is shown below:

Your Hand

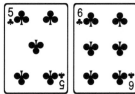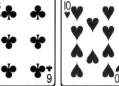

The Flop

Here you've flopped a King-high flush draw. It's a little better draw because you'll make your flush just a hair more often than you'd fill an open-end straight (35 percent vs. 32 percent of the time), but mostly because a flush will beat a straight whenever both hands are made in the same pot. With either hand, though, you have an attractive, playable situation worth pursuing. The most sterile way to play these hands is to just call and see if you hit. But if you're in late position, there is often something to be gained by getting a little fancier. The flush draw illustration offers the more vivid example of this.

Your K/J of clubs above provides not only a draw to a flush, but also two overcards to the board. If there's a bet, you should probably raise. That will often induce your opponents to check to you on the next card. If that turn card was any King, Jack or club (15 cards), you'll have made either the top pair, or a flush, and you can just keep right on betting as if your were always going to anyway. If you miss you can:

1. Bet again if there appears to be some chance your opponent may not want to call the larger 4th Street bet.
2. Just check along.

If you make the first play, you might win the pot without having to hit your hand. Yet if your opponent calls, you have a legitimate play. If you make the second play, you will have gotten to see 4th and 5th Streets for two small bets (i.e. a $30 call and a $30 raise in a $30/$60 game) instead of one small and one big bet ($30 on the flop and $60 the turn).

If your opponent is a tough player, however, he's likely to have seen this move before and may just call your raise on the flop and then bet right into you again on the turn if a "blank" comes. So it's going to be up to you to judge just what you (as always) can get away with.

Concept #51: Flopping a Secondary Draw

There are also two basic types of secondary draws you can hit on the flop. The first would be:

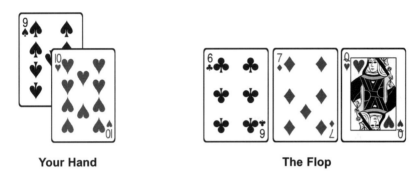

Your Hand   **The Flop**

This is a common example of a "gut shot." You need an inside 8 to make a straight. It's a longshot. It's usually not worth pursuing, but if you're practically sure you can get in for just one bet, and it's a multi-way pot, you can call to see the turn card, then give it up if you've missed. Now, let's look at an even more remote type of secondary draw:

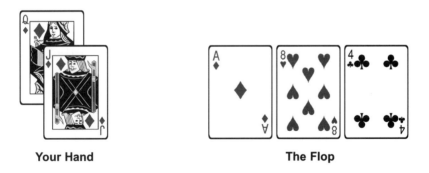

Your Hand   **The Flop**

You've essentially missed the flop with your suited connectors; however, you do have a "back door" flush draw. That means if a diamond comes on both the turn and the river you'll have a flush. It's a 23-to-1 shot. These should almost always be given up. You'd need to be able to get in for one bet in a five- or six-way pot that was raised up before the flop to make it worthwhile, and that opportunity is seldom available.

Sometimes, however, you can have other outs with your back door draw that can make it worth taking a card off on the flop. For instance, let's reverse the Queen and the Ace in the example on the previous page. If you held the A/J of diamonds and the flop was Qd/8h/4c, then 13 turn cards would give you either the top pair or a flush draw. That would usually make calling one bet (but not a raise) worthwhile in a healthy-sized pot.

Concept #52: When Rags Flop

Other than flopping a pair or a draw, there are hardly any other situations worth playing beyond the flop in Hold'em. If the pot is multi-way, either you flop something or you're done with it. Normally, you must live by that rule.

If the action is heads-up, however, and the flop is all small, unrelated cards (known as "rags"), then high cards alone do have some value. Suppose, for example, that you raised coming in with A/Q and got just one caller behind you. The flop comes down:

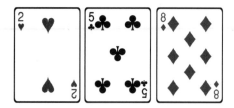

You missed completely, but what could your lone opponent have called your raise with? If it wasn't a pocket pair, you most likely still have the best hand since he shouldn't be calling with a deuce, 5, or 8 in his hand. Here, you should probably bet to avoid giving a free card. If you get called and another small card comes on the turn (9 or lower with no pair), you'll have to judge your opponent's playing style. If he'll usually call the small bet on the flop with almost anything, but will fold for the big bet on the turn if he's still empty, then you should bet again. But if he's the cautious type who needs to flop a hand to put any further money in the pot, then you're probably already beat and should check on the turn and fold if he bets.

Now, what if the tables were completely reversed? I mean, your opponent came in raising, and you called behind him with A/Q; then he bet on the flop when the 2/5/8 fell. He's trying to suggest to you that he already has a hand—and he very well might. Bear in mind, however, that if he was really strong, such as with pocket Aces or Kings he might have checked, looking for bigger action later in the hand. So he probably has either a moderately big pair or a hand similar to yours.

Again, this is where you must be able to anticipate your opponent's reactions. What would he do if you raised him here, regardless of which hand he held? If he'd just call whether he has two high cards or something like pocket 10s, and would be likely to check to you on the turn, you can go ahead and raise him on the flop because you'll probably get to see both 4th and 5th Streets for those two small bets, rather than one small and one big. This you'll accomplish by checking behind him on 4th Street unless an Ace or Queen comes, in which case you'll, of course, bet for value.

However, the more savvy players are used to this tactic and will call your raise. Then if 4th Street turns up another blank and they do have the pocket pair (or might be on the "muscle"), they'll bet right out again. If this is likely to be your opponent's course of action, you would have been better off to just call on the flop. In either case, though, if you're still empty on the turn, you shouldn't put any more money into the pot. Just check along if you can or fold if he bets, unless he's playing wildly.

If you both check on the turn and he bets out at the river (provided another blank comes), once again it's judgment time. He may have been waiting on 4th Street to check/raise you with a huge pair, or he might be trying to steal the pot now with something like K/Q since you showed weakness by checking behind him on the turn. Most opponents will just check two high cards here hoping to win in a showdown. But if this player has exhibited some tendencies towards bluffing thus far, you'd probably better take the 5- or 6-to-1 pot odds and call.

Be aware that there is one key scare card you don't want to see at the river in this last scenario, and that's a King. If the dreaded Cowboy does come out and your opponent bets, there are just too many ways you can now be beaten. Surrender! If he bluffed you, he bluffed you. This will have been one of those rare times when it's actually better to be in early position, where the first player to put money in the pot wins it.

Concept #53: Totaling Your "Outs"

Many times you've come all the way to 4th Street and you know you don't have a winning hand yet; but you do have a straight draw, a flush draw, or maybe middle pair with a gut-shot straight draw, etc. You're pretty sure if you improve your hand, you'll win, but how do you know whether it's worth calling to try? This, you'll determine by totaling your "outs." Every single card in the deck that will make you a winning hand is considered an "out." In general, *you need about six outs to make your hand worth drawing to when there's one more card to come.*

The above is merely an "average" statement. In small heads-up pots, or if it'll cost a bet and a raise, you need more outs than that. And in big pots you may not need as many.

Here's an example of a very typical situation. Suppose you have J/10 offsuit and on the turn the board is:

Any 8 or King at the river will give you the stone nuts (sure winner). What are your chances? Going strictly by what you can see, you have eight "outs" or eight cards that will make your straight among 46 unseen cards. Mathematically, that's just about a 5-to-1 shot. With the six or seven big bets that are usually already in the pot, plus another bet or two you'll win if you hit your hand, you'll get about 8-to-1 odds on your call. Hence, your eight outs are more than enough to gamble with.

Fact is, most open-end straight draws and flush draws are easily worth a call on the turn in Hold'em. Identifying your outs in this situation is very clear and your pot odds are there. The only times this isn't true is when the pot is very small or you might hit your hand and still lose.

Much more troublesome, however, are those lesser hands, like second pair with a gut shot, that make your decision more blurry. Here's one of them. You have the 7/8 of hearts and the 4th Street board is:

You originally flopped middle pair with a back-door flush draw and back-door straight draw, so you called. Your flush potential died when the 10 of spades came on the turn, but now a gut-shot 9 will make you a straight. Somebody bets, there's a call and you're last. Is your hand worth a call? This is tricky. All in all, there are nine cards that will improve your hand (four 9s, two 8s and three 7s), but how many of them will win for you? That is, how many actual winning "outs" do you really have?

Well, if one of the two remaining 8s comes at the river, your trips will most likely take the pot. We'll count those as two winning outs.

Next, if a 7 comes giving you two pair, anybody holding a 9 will have a straight. It's not likely that a 9 is out there against you, but it's not unrealistic. You'll win with 8s and 7s maybe two-thirds of the times that a 7 comes on the end. So let's figure you for two more outs with the 7 and write off that third 7 as a loser. Now you're up to about four outs.

Finally, what if the 9 comes to make you a straight? This might very well be big trouble since anybody with a Jack will have a higher straight! And some very plausible hands out against you with this board might be J/Q, J/10, J/9, or even J/J. I'd be pretty leery to count any 9s among my winning outs—*maybe* one. Assessing it this way, it seems you have about a four or five-outer—and that fifth out just might cost you a lot of money if you hit it. That's not good enough unless the pot is bigger than usual. Yet, there can't be too many players in it because extra players would make it even more likely that somebody out there has a Jack.

Here's where you need to be perceptive when totaling up your outs. If some of your alleged outs end up beating you, what appeared to be a one bet proposition might turn out to cost you three bets!

Concept #54: Top Pair at the River

On average, smaller hands win the pot in Hold'em than in 7 Stud. More often than not, *top pair* will take the money. There will be plenty of times, however, when this probably won't be the case. You don't need me to point out the obvious ones such as when there's a four-flush on board, or something such as two pair plus a high three-card straight-flush. Still, you ought to get a feel for whether your top pair is good and if you should bet it for value, make a crying call, or toss it into the muck.

The thing to remember is that you shouldn't see disaster in every dangerous card that falls. As I said, Hold'em is a smaller hand game than that. When the flop comes with two spades and a third spade hits on the river, there just won't be a flush out there all that often, particularly if the pot is short-handed. Following are some mathematically threatening boards that realistically are probably not anything to worry about if you have top pair.

This board has a pair and, technically, anyone holding a 7 has trips. Practically speaking though, what would anyone be hanging around past the flop with a 7 in their hand for? If you've got a King with a pretty good kicker, you should probably bet for value. Here's one more probable false alarm:

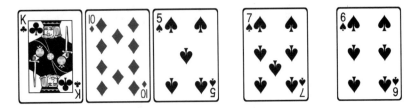

Similar story here. There's both a possible straight and a possible flush out there. Still, neither is likely since it all developed beyond the flop. There aren't a whole lot of cards that somebody would have called a bet on the flop with that fit in with the turn and the river cards. Both of these examples show that the sequence in which the cards came out are often more important than the cards themselves. Now, here are a couple of flops that you should be very wary of if you have top pair:

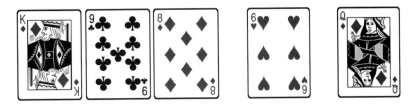

Here, anybody with two diamonds would most likely stay to the river, giving them a flush. Also, somebody holding a commonly played hand like J/10 would almost certainly stick it out, making a straight. You can even be beaten by an ordinary Q/9. If you have, say, K/J and have more than one opponent, you almost can't bet it. If it's bet to you, there's a good chance you're beat, but your judgment of the bettor's playing habits should be the prevailing determinant in whether you call. If he's been known to bluff when a three-flush hits the board (representing a flush), by calling is how you might gain a value bet with your top pair. Here's one last development which more than likely has just beaten your top pair:

There are a flock of plausible opponents' hands that will beat you here. An A/10, Q/10, or J/10 will all make trips. Both a Q/J or a 7/8 will have already had a straight (though you'd probably have heard from them on the turn). Plus, a host of other suited hands like the A/Q of clubs, A/J of clubs, A/9 of clubs, Q/9 of clubs, J/9 of clubs, or 8/9 of clubs all will have backed into a flush. For your K/J, this is basically a "check and call" or "check and fold" hand depending upon the number of players and your reading ability. Against two or three opponents though, your top pair is probably—to put it bluntly—*dogmeat*.

In summary, even though top pair will often win the pot, it most likely won't when the board contains closely knit high cards that can form a number of straights.

Chapter 7

7 Stud Hi/Lo Split (8 or Better)

The game 7 Stud Hi/Lo split is a popular one in casino card rooms and is played with an 8 qualifier on the low side. That means, to win the low half of the pot your hand must be an 8 or lower, lest the high hand gets it all.

Hi/Lo Stud-8 or Better is often integrated into "combination" games in which three or four poker variants are played in rotation at one table. As a "stand-alone" game, it's not all that often played for low-level stakes. The premiere card rooms of California usually spread daily Stud-8 or Better games of $15/$30 or $20/$40. Elsewhere during major tournaments, $30/$60, $50/$100, and $75/$150 Stud-8 or Better can usually be found in the side games. Stud-8 is a game that has many traps for the unseasoned player. The first and most important trap to avoid is:

Concept #55: Playing for Half the Pot

One of the primary fundamentals to understand about any Hi/Lo split poker game is that playing strictly for half the pot is a losing strategy. What's the reason? Let's use a typical hand of $50/$100 Stud-8 or better as an example.

Eight players ante $10 apiece and the low card brings it in for $15. That makes roughly a $100 pot before anybody plays their hands. Somebody will ordinarily raise it to $50 and maybe there will be four total gamblers going to the turn (4th Street). Now the pot is at $300. On 4th Street, some players will improve their hands and some won't, but maybe three contestants will remain to see 5th Street with $450 in the pot thus far. Then on 5th Street things often become heads-up because of the double-sized bet. With a bet/call the rest of the way by each of the two finalists, this pot will finish up at $1,050. Splitting that two ways, each winner will get back $525 after putting in $400. That's a $125 profit. Well, you don't have to be a math major to figure out that if you play four hands, successfully split three of them and lose the other, you are $25 behind. *If you never scooped a whole pot, you'd typically have to bat better than .750 with your splits to break even.*

Few one-way hands are a 3-to-1 favorite at the start. That's why when you're selecting a starting hand, you want to pick holdings that can go both ways. And what kind of holding would that be? Ideally, of course, you'd love to have something like an A/2/3 suited. That's a super-premium starting hand in Stud-8 or Better. It can make a low, it can make a straight or a flush, and it can also pair the Ace to make the highest pair. But let's be realistic. That starting hand will only come along once every 5,500 hands.

I'm afraid you're going to have to find a whole repertoire of other Stud-8 or Better hands to play, but which ones? That brings us to our second big trap in Stud-8 or Better, namely that:

Concept #56: You Can't Re-Route an All High Hand

It turns out that even though you need an "8" low minimum to win the low half, Stud-8 or Better still favors playing low hands over high hands. To illustrate this as vividly as possible, take a look at the two starting hands below:

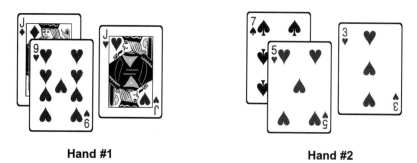

Hand #1   **Hand #2**

Now, a starting pair of Jacks may end up winning the high half of the pot and it may not. It might even win the whole pot when nobody makes an 8 low. But the really important thing is that those two Jacks with a 9 kicker can never, ever win the low. That's huge!

Now let's look at the 7/5/3. It's a pretty good start for low, but that's not all by any means. Even though it's not a classic low-straight draw, every once in a while it'll still turn into a 7-high straight which is a darned good high and low at the same time. Another overlooked thing that can happen with a low start is that when it misses its low, it often misses by pairing. If it pairs a couple of times it'll beat those two Jacks more often than the Jacks would care to remember. And don't forget, it's a seven card game. A pretty fair number of pots have been won both ways with a hand like:

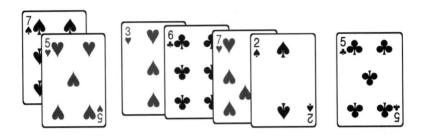

That's two pair and a 7 low. And lastly, the 7/5/3 could get lucky, make a flush, and still make a low. Because of the immensely greater versatility that a low hand has, you should fold the majority of your high hands in Stud-8 or Better. That's a tough fact to get used to, particularly if your "A" game is 7 Stud High, and it's all because any low start could win high—but an all-high start can never win low.

Concept #57: High Pairs Are at a Huge Playing Disadvantage

Concept #57 is axiomatic. It will bring itself to bear on your high pairs again and again while you're playing one. Picture yourself in the Stud-8 or Better hand below:

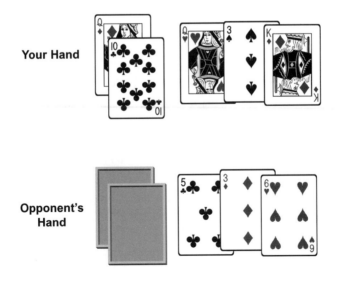

You raised coming in, bet again on 4th Street and the 5 quietly called both bets. Now what? If he's made a low, the best you can do is get your money back plus half the antes and bring-in. If he has a straight or makes a straight, you're virtually dead. If he's made two concealed pair or trips, you're an underdog to get any part of the pot, and he can still make a low. Yet, the least a rational opponent will have here is a small pair with a low draw. There's almost no way he doesn't have a playable hand against you, but you may very well not have a playable hand against him.

Can you see how your hand is paralyzed? You just can't know whether to "poop or go blind," so folding might very well be the most sensible thing to do. It could be worse. What if his board were a two-suited 5/6/7 or 5/4/3? Now you definitely have to give him the pot even though he might only have something like 2-6/5-6-7. You may have the best hand, yet you have to lay it down. Your opponent, however, knows just about where you're at and can play his hand quite effectively.

That's how handcuffed you are when you play an obvious high hand in this game. When you get to 5th Street and your opponent has three low cards, you're at his mercy! He gets to decide how the hand will be played. If he needs a free card, he can probably finagle it. If his low is made, he can bet with impunity. If he's got a low plus a straight draw or flush draw, he's "freerolling" at your end of the pot. Going by strict mathematical odds, a high pair on 3rd Street is the favorite over a semi-flexible three-card low, *but the low hand has such a betting advantage that it all works out the other way around*. If the low start catches a high card on 4th Street, he'll fold and get away from his hand cheaply. The high pair, however, is usually tied on to his hand, very often to the bitter end. Wouldn't you rather sit on the other side of the table, be more in control, and even take down a few pots with the worst hand?

Still and all, this is not to say that you can never play a high pair in Stud-8 or Better—although most of them should be mucked at the start. The critical thing to recognize is that:

Concept #58: All High Pairs Are Not Created Equal

There are three key factors that can make your high pair playable in Stud-8 or Better. Any one of them will often do the trick.

1. If it's a pair of Aces.
2. If it's buried with a low upcard.
3. If you have nearly perfect position.

Factor #1: This should be obvious. A pair of Aces is much better than a pair of Kings in this game. With the Kings, any low hand that contains an Ace will knock you off if he happens to pair it, not so if you have Aces.

Factor #2: Take a look at the two hands below:

Hand A

Hand B

If you play hand A, everybody in the world knows you have a high hand, probably a pair of Queens. Your opponent(s) will yield if they blank on the turn and put on the pressure if they make a low on 5th Street. But if you have hand B, they are likely to figure you for a low hand. This will allow you some playing latitude that you wouldn't ordinarily have. Against hand "B" your opponent may keep coming when he should tend to fold and vice versa.

Possible examples of hand B's superiority are numerous, but just think what's likely to happen if on 5th Street you have Q-Q/6-4-9 while your opponent shows ?-?/3-7-7. Or what if you have Q-Q/6-4-4, while he shows ?-?/3-7-9? Or suppose you have Q-Q/6-5-4 against an opponent showing ?-?/3-7-8. That 6 door card of yours (rather than a Queen) makes your strong hands look weaker and your weak hands look stronger—which plays to your advantage. That's why you can usually play hand B, but very seldom hand A.

Factor #3: Now suppose a deuce brings it in three seats to your left, everybody folds up to you and there's just a 9 and a Jack still left to act. Well, it's 2-to-1 against the deuce having two other low cards in the hole. Besides that, the Jack or the 9 have high hands if they have anything at all—so now you're in great shape even with hand A and should raise it up! If you are ever going to play a split high pair lower than Aces, you need conditions practically as good as those described above. Don't learn this lesson the hard, expensive way. When a deuce brings it in, a 5 calls, a 3 calls, then it's up to you with a King, or, worse yet, an Ace behind you, muck your 9-Q/Q as fast as you can! With that point having been hammered home, let's move onto defining and ranking a set of playable starting hands for 7 Stud-8 or Better.

Concept #59: Stud-8 or Better Starting Hands

Some bonafide Stud-8 or Better starting hands are just about always good to play, and some others are highly situational such as with the high pair example in Concept #58. Let's run them down, beginning with the best of the best.

1. ROLLED UP TRIPS: Being dealt something like 5-5/5 on your first three cards is about as nice a start as you'll ever get. Strangely enough though, it's not a two-way hand (practically speaking). Remember my mentioning that most high hands aren't 3-to-1 favorites at the start? Well, a roll-up is an exception!

When you get one of these, you should push it as hard as possible. This means raising and re-raising right on 3rd Street, whether you have trip Kings or trip deuces. The reason you cut loose so early with a roll-up in Stud-8 or Better is that you want desperately to discourage low hands from seeing 5th Street and maybe taking half the pot away from you. Remember, you win four or five times as much by scooping a pot as by splitting it. Winning all of a $200 pot will usually net you more profit than getting half of a $500 pot, so don't be afraid to end it too soon.

2. LOW STRAIGHT/FLUSH: A hand like the A/2/3 of hearts or the 3/4/5 of clubs has enormous potential. You can come in raising and often even re-raising since you'll be taking off another card even when you miss on the turn. If several of your suit and straight cards are out, however, you should play it more quietly since, after all, you have nothing unless you improve.

Stepsisters of a straight/flush wheel start are hands like a suited 5/6/7. Often these can also be played pretty fast out of the gate since they don't blank out both ways very often. You'll go past 5th Street with the vast majority of all these starts.

3. PAIR of ACES with LOW KICKER: The thing to understand is that there are really three classes of paired Aces on 3rd Street in this game.

Class A—Whenever you pick up a starting hand like 6-A/A or A-A/6 (low kicker), you've got the green light to go ahead and start jamming. You'll make Aces up or better 60 percent of the time, and with your small kicker you'll even make a low 20 percent of the time, plus your hand is somewhat disguised. Two Aces are much stronger when your kicker is an 8 or lower and it doesn't make a heck of a lot of difference whether the Aces are split or buried. Just start pounding the pot.

Class B—Now, when you have Aces with a big kicker, you'd much rather have J-A/A (Class "B"), than A-A/J (Class C) because with the Ace up, the four-card lows may give up on 5th Street if you now show something like ?/?/A-7-4. But with the Jack up, no low draws will fear you and you wish they'd get out. Class B Aces (split) should be started out aggressively, but don't go crazy with raises because your hand can get a lot weaker by 5th Street.

Class C—Buried Aces with a big upcard like A-A/J is actually a pretty tentative hand that can cost you a lot of money. You should play it fast only if you're pretty sure you can trim the field short. And remember, you'll be trying to accomplish that with something like a Jack for a door card. In many cases, you should just quietly call on 3rd Street. Sometimes you'll get the opportunity to check/raise a couple of players out of the pot on the turn, and other times you'll just quietly fold on 5th Street because things didn't shape up right. Don't trap yourself with this hand.

4. LOW THREE-STRAIGHTS and THREE-FLUSHES: Hands like 4/5/6 offsuit and the 2/4/7 of hearts are highly desirable starts. They're versatile and come along a lot more often than a suited three-straight. You can just about always put in the first raise with them and often re-raise if they're pretty live. Unless your cards fall quite dead on the turn, or somebody makes something ominous, or the betting gets very rich, you'll go right to 5th Street even when you blank on 4th Street.

5. LOW PAIR with ACE KICKER: An overlooked and underrated Stud-8 or Better hand is something like A-6/6. You're not too thrilled with it in a multi-way field when you're up against both high and low door cards. But heads-up it plays very favorably against either a low start or against a high pair lower than Aces.

Heads up against split Queens you've got the playability of the Ace overcard for high, plus additional outs for low, combined with a puzzling board that gives you commanding leverage in the play of the hand. Heads-up against something like a 2/5/6, you've got a head start on the high end, and should you lose that you'll sometimes escape with the low. The down side comes when you're up against both the split Queens and the 2/5/6 at the same time. Here, you'll start out chasing in both directions and will have to release it if there's a double raise on 3rd Street, or if you blank on the turn, or if you haven't made two pair by 5th Street if an opponent shows three low cards.

6. LOW PAIR with LOW KICKER: A weak sister of hand #5 would be the likes of a 6/7/7. Not having the Ace to pair here matters quite a bit. It's also fairly valuable to have either two straight cards or a two-flush, or both. Even then, however, you almost have to be heads-up with either a high pair or a low hand and should muck it right on the turn if you catch a 9 through King. If it looks as if the pot is going to be multi-way at the outset, just toss this hand into the muck.

7. FACE CARD PAIRS: Concepts #57 and #58 illustrate the many pitfalls of playing a hand like 9-Q/Q. If it's a split pair, the exposed picture card pigeonholes your hand. Opponents can play rings around you. Fold these 90 percent of the time.

If your face-card pair is buried such as with Q-Q/9, it's just a little different. If you make trips you'll get action and if you pair your door card you'll get a lot of respect. You can often take a card or two off with these hands, but don't come in raising without great position as they can sour too quickly.

The most viable kind of face-card pair is one that's buried with a small upcard such as Q-Q/5. You still have all the power of a big pair, plus your opponents don't know where you're at, and you do actually have an outside shot at a low hand. You should come in raising with these as long as you're quite sure it's the best high hand out and you're not going to be up against an Ace.

8. WIDE THREE-CARD LOWS: Routine low starts like 7/5/2 or 8/6/4 that can't, or *almost* can't, make a straight, do have their place in the game but not very often. One time you might play them is when you are the bring-in and are facing a "position" raise from a lone opponent. On another occasion, you might go ahead and raise the bring-in if it's come down to just you and him, or if there's nothing but a 9 or a 10 left to act. Finally, you can usually limp in with a wide three-card low in late position when there's no raise. Otherwise, muck them.

SUMMARY: While playing Stud-8 or better, you'll be tempted to play many other starting hands not described here. Something like a J/Q/K with two diamonds or a K-10/3 of spades will look good to you, but remember that these are merely one-way drawing hands that might also make a big pair. That just doesn't cut it in a split pot game. About the only "off" type high hand you might sometimes consider would be an A/Q/4 suited or a 4/Q/A suited—but not an A/4/Q suited. You have to have that high card buried to hide its inherent weakness. On the low side, other "off" hands like 2/5/8 with no straight or flush potential just don't have enough flexibility going for them. These should be mucked in the vast majority of circumstances.

Concept #60: Low Stud Hand Drawing Odds

It's surprising how much catching one low card or one high card will affect your chances to make a low hand. The following table outlines the odds to improve your Stud hand for low. These odds have been rounded off for easy digestion.

Familiarizing yourself with them will give you a good feel for where you stand with various low draws at different stages of the hand.

Low Hand Odds

You Have	Make an 8 Low or Better
On 3rd Street	
A/3/5	even money
A/3/K	4-to-1 underdog
A/Q/K	23-to-1 underdog
On 4th Street	
A/3/5/2	2.5-to-1 favorite
A/3/5/K	2-to-1 underdog
A/2/Q/K	13-to-1 underdog
On 5th Street	
A/3/5/2/K	1.33-to-1 favorite
A/3/5/Q/K	6-to-1 underdog
On 6th Street	
A/3/5/2/Q/K	2-to-1 underdog

Concept #61: Playing the Turn

Fourth Street (the turn) in Stud-8 or Better is a much more decisive juncture than in high-only Stud, particularly if you have a low hand. Here are some typical examples.

LOW HAND/BUST: In most cases if you start out with three lows and catch a "brick" (9 through King) on the turn, you're done with it. What's the reason? The picture on the following page tells the whole story.

The percentages beneath each hand show how often you'll make a low if you play to the river. If all you have is a three-card low with no significant high potential, you've got nothing. Get out.

LOW HAND/SEMI-BUST: Now, instead, if you had something like a 4-5/7-K and the King gave you three dia-

Case A

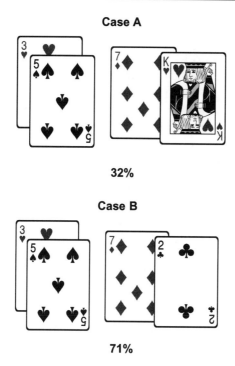

32%

Case B

71%

monds, you didn't miss entirely if the 6s and diamonds are still pretty live. Here, you could probably call a bet (but not a raise) and take a card off against one high and one mediocre low board.

LOW HAND/PAIR: There will also be times when you start out with that 3-5/7 (from the preceding picture) against a face-card and, on the turn, you pair up. If you've made a concealed pair such as 3-5/7-5, the high board will usually bet and you can call if it's heads up, or if you're pretty sure it won't get raised behind you.

If you paired your door card as in 3-5/7-7 and are heads-up against a high board, bet out! He almost can't raise you and he might fold. Even when he doesn't fold, lots of good things can happen for you on 5th Street.

Now when you've got that paired door card and the pot's three way against both a high and a low board, the situation becomes delicate. It would be huge for you if you could knock the high board out! Yet, if you can't, your hand is worth a crying call at best. Therefore, if the betting order goes—*you, high board, low board*—then you should check, since the high board may be afraid to bet into both a paired door card and a low draw. If the low board then bets, check/raise the high board forcing him to call two cold bets from a paired door card, or fold. If, however, the high board bets and the low board calls, give it a crying call. And if the high board bets, then the low board raises, give it up.

Now with those same hands if the betting order goes —*you, low board, high board*—go ahead and bet. After the low board acts, the high will most likely either fold or just call to see what happens on 5th Street.

ROUGH LOW DRAW: When you're in a three-way pot on 4th Street against one high and one low board, if you caught an 8 while the other low board caught lower, give up unless the low hand is a very loose player. You can't continue to play holding the short end of the low possibilities when the high half is already spoken for.

HIGH PAIR: If you've got a pair of Kings on the turn against two opponents who both catch something that looks like the picture below:

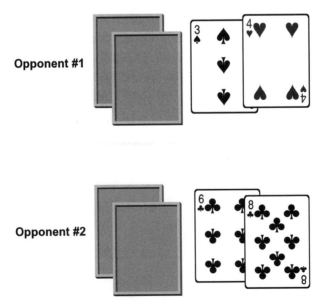

you should check and fold if there's a bet. You'll practically be playing in the blind the whole rest of the way. If they both have low draws, it's about 7-to-1 against them both missing. If one of them has a pair, a straight draw or a flush draw you're in a dog fight—probably for half a pot. Remember, a straight draw or flush draw can make it's high and it's low at the same time. If you've already made a second pair, however, bet it and see what develops on 5th Street.

HIGH PAIR vs. ACE: Another time you should probably release your Kings on the turn is when a low opponent catches an Ace. If it didn't pair him, he's a 5-to-2 favorite to take the low half of the pot away from you. If it did, you're a 2-to-1 dog for the high and he can still escape with the low. If it's a three-way pot you have even more problems. These are the crippling pitfalls of playing high pairs in this game. If things become unfriendly on the turn, you must throw your hand away right there.

Concept #62: 5th Street

At this point in the hand, most situations are either heads up or three way. You'll have to make some pivotal, critical decisions here since this is where the real money starts going into the pot. Let's look at the more common problem scenarios.

LOW DRAW vs. HIGH HAND: Many times you'll start with a three-card low, make a fourth low on the turn, then catch a useless 10 or some other "brick" on 5th Street— and will be heads up against an obvious high hand as shown on the following page.

When the high hand bets, should you chase, trying to escape with a low? In a typical sized pot, the answer is yes, since you'll get there four times out of seven on average. So long as there was the customary raise and at least three-way action on 3rd Street, you'll get enough money back when you make your low to more than cover the times you miss. If the

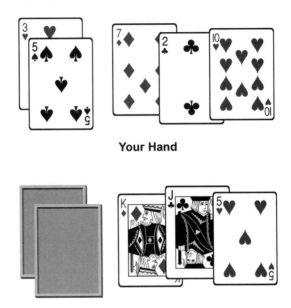

Your Hand

Your Opponent's Hand

pot was heads-up right from the get-go, however, and there were no re-raises, or many of your needed low cards are dead, you should fold.

LOW DRAW with THREE-WAY POT: Now what if the pot is still three way on 5th Street when you have that low draw? Well, if the third player has a high hand too, you've got a very easy call. But if the third hand has a low draw with you, you should generally fold—unless there was at least one extra raise somewhere earlier in the hand. Then, due to the three additional small bets you'll split when you win, you should call if your low draw is about as good as your opponent's.

Note: There's one other thing you should think about in this three-way situation with a basic-sized pot. If you think your low opponent will fold if you call, and he should to avoid merely sharing a shot at the low, then by all means call. That way, you'll get to go heads-up with the high hand after the other low draw leaves some dead money in the pot. But if he'll just call behind you, in which case your own low chances will have become too slim, or if he's already called in front of you—then fold. This is one of those unusual spots where acting first and calling puts the onus of folding on the later position low draw.

LOW DRAW with SMALL PAIR in a THREE-WAY POT: Sometimes in a three-way pot you'll have a hand like 2-6/3-7-7 and your two opponents will be showing:

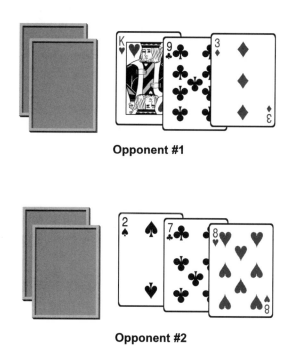

Opponent #1

Opponent #2

It's pretty clear that you're behind both ways, but are you close enough to keep playing? As long as the high hand has no open pair and you're drawing to a better low than your low opponent can already have, go ahead and call. But you must have those two factors going for you.

If, however, you've paired your door card (such as with 2-6/3-7-3) but still have the same hand, a check/raise by you may knock the high hand out, which would be all to your advantage. Be careful though. You'll have to anticipate how your high opponent will react before trying that move, lest you end up wasting your own money.

SMOOTH LOW DRAW vs. a HIGH HAND and a MADE 8 LOW: Other times you'll have a good low draw like 2-3/4-7-Q and find yourself up against one obvious high hand and another player with an apparent rough 8 made. In order to keep coming in this spot, your low draw must be a 7-4, no worse and the 8 low you're chasing must be an 8-7, otherwise fold, unless your low draw contains a live Ace that might win high simply by pairing it. Then you could call with a 7-4 draw against an 8-6 made, or with a 7-5 draw against an 8-7 made.

HIGH PAIR vs. a COORDINATED LOW BOARD: A revolting development when you start with a big pair is getting to 5th Street and looking across the table at something like a ?-?/4-5-6 or maybe a ?-?/3-6-8, all suited. Not to beat a dead horse, but this is one of the many disadvantages of playing a big pair to begin with in this game. When this happens, you've got too many ways to lose so get out. If you've already made a second pair, though, you probably have to keep coming since you can beat two small pair and after all, you might even fill up.

HIGH PAIR vs. a LOW PAIRED DOOR CARD: Suppose you've still got two Kings on 5th Street and are heads-up against:

Being high on board, your opponent bets right out. The thing of it is, he's not as likely to have trips as he would be if this was regular 7 Card Stud because in high only, he wouldn't have played three unpaired low cards. In straight Stud, he'd have trips about eight times out of 20 in this spot. But in Stud-8 or Better, he'll have them only about three times in 20 (because of all the low hands he'd start with). The chart below tells you how many times out of 20 a decent player will have each of his feasible playing hands when he pairs that low door card on 5th Street. At the far right are your odds of winning the high half of the pot against each hand.

He'll Have	This Often	Your Odds to Win High
four lows with pair	10 times	2-to-1 favorite
four lows with pair + straight potential	3 times	even money
two pair	4 times	2-to-1 underdog
trips	3 times	11-to-1 underdog

Crunch all those numbers together and on average, you'll split the pot about one fourth of the time, scoop it a fourth of the time, and get scooped half the time. You're definitely in a weaker position than your opponent. If this had happened on 4th Street, the pot would have been smaller and you'd just release your hand. But here on 5th Street your pot odds usually make it right to check and call. Remember, if he doesn't have trips or two pair (and he usually won't), you either won't have to call a bet on every street—or he'll be semi-bluffing into you without the best high hand.

Note: One thing that could make you fold your big pair in this spot is if your opponent is the type who wouldn't be likely to bet unless he has the two pair or trips. If you could be pretty sure that's what you're up against, you'd have to fold. Also note that a high paired door card such as ?-?/Q-9-Q is even more likely to be trips than in straight high Stud. That's because in Stud-8 or Better, so many 3-flushes and small buried pairs are folded at the start.

HIGH PAIR vs. two apparent MADE LOWS: When the pot's three way on 5th Street and you've got the big pair against two low boards, it's important how versatile their low boards look. If they only have:

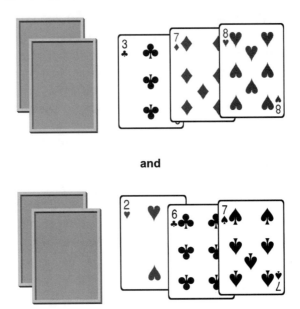

you can probably play onward. But if you're staring at:

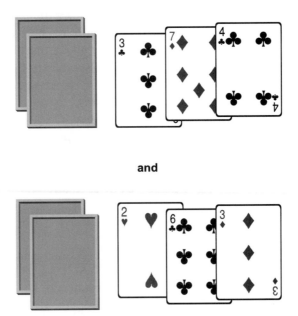

there are just too many high hands that can be made to beat you and you have to fold. Those 5th Street cards knocked you out of the box! Even if just one of the low boards showed a three-flush while the other showed a rough unsuited 8, your hand wouldn't be worth pursuing. You just can't take the pressure in these spots. Once again, though, if you've already made a big two pair you're going to be stuck playing this hand out and hoping you don't get beat.

Concept #63: The Best Hand in a Three-Way Pot

All the 5th Street situations described in Concept #62 involve "trouble" hands and whether they should be played any further. An even trickier concept to understand about the nature of Hi/Lo Split is whether you should raise when you have the best hand going in your direction—while a third player is drawing at the other half. Some say you should always raise to punish those chasing you—yet others insist you should keep the betting down because you're laying 2-1 odds on every new bet (i.e. if you and two other players put $100 apiece into the pot and you win half, you'll get back $150 for a $50 profit—but it will cost $100 if you lose).

So what's the right play? It depends! Sometimes you'll have the best high hand against another high hand and a low. Other times you'll have the best low hand against another low hand and a high. Since a picture is worth a thousand words, look at the illustration on the following page:

Situations related to this come up all the time in Hi/Lo split. You started with a low three-flush and made your flush on five. Your high opponent, however, came in raising on 3rd Street and has now paired his door card making trip Queens his most likely hand. Unlike pairing a low door card in Stud-8 or Better, a high-paired door card usually means trips since there aren't many other high hands he would have played. Fearlessly, he bets out. You almost certainly have the best

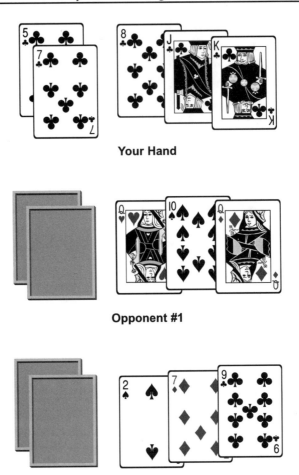

Your Hand

Opponent #1

Opponent #2

hand at the moment. But even when your flush holds up for high, somebody else (the low draw) is threatening to take half the pot away from you. So should you raise or just call? In this particular case, the key is that the low hand isn't there yet. He's still trying to make a low; therefore the other half of the pot remains up in the air. And nearly 30 percent of the time, that low money will go to you. Because of that, you have more equity in this pot than anybody else. If the low was already made, the tables would be turned and you should just call. But as it stands, you should raise.

Here's how that all works. When the pot is three way with both ends still in question, anybody who puts in money with less than a 66 percent shot at half loses equity with each additional bet. So where do these three players stand in this scenario? Why don't we just play the hand out 21 times and see who ends up with what? We'll assume the stakes are $50/$100. With three players in the hand from the get-go, the early pot will contain about $400. After a $100 bet on 5th, 6th, and 7th Streets, each pot will finish up at either $1,200 or $1,300 (depending upon whether the low draw makes his low). But if there's a bet and a raise on each of those Streets, the final pot will be either $2,000 or $2,200. Who benefits and who gets hurt by the raises?

Let's look at the low board first, since it's the simplest to analyze. Practically speaking, when he makes his low he gets half the pot (except for those rare occasions when he makes his low, but is beaten by a better low in your own hand). When he misses, he loses—end of story. A four-card low on 5th Street will get there about four times out of seven or 57 percent of the time. So basically, he'll win half the pot 12 times in our 21-hand sample. With a bet on each Street, but no raises, the low will get back $650 twelve times (netting a $350 profit on each win) and will lose $200 the other nine times (since he won't call at the river when he misses). But if he's forced to put in two bets on every street, he'll net $500 on each split and every loss will cost $400. That all shakes out like this:

	Splits	Scoops	Losers	Net per Hand
Bet Only	12 @ +$350	None	9 @ -$200	+$114 avg.
Bet & Raise	12 @ +$500	None	9 @ -$400	+$114 avg.

You can see here that raising doesn't benefit the low draw, so it has to help somebody else.

How about the other high hand? Let's just assume he does have three Queens. In that case, he'll fill up one-third of the time, or seven times out of 21. But he'll do a bit better than just get half the pot those seven times. That's because three of those seven times, the low draw will miss his low. In an unraised pot, his scoops would net $900 apiece. Each scoop in a raised pot would net $1,400. Here's his breakdown:

	Splits	Scoops	Losers	Net per Hand
Bet Only	4 @ +$350	3 @ +$900	14 @ -$300	-$5 avg.
Bet & Raise	4 @ +$500	3 @ +$1,400	14 @ -$600	-$105 avg.

Here, the extra bets really hurt the second best high hand big time. If he could've read where he was at, he shouldn't have even called because those extra bets overrode his pre-existing pot odds, turning his hand into a losing play. Where's all that additional money going?

Let's look at your flush. It'll hold up for high against those trips two-thirds of the time, or 14 out of 21 times. Of your 14 wins, the low will take the other half away eight times and your flush will scoop the pot those six times that the low draw misses. Depending upon the betting, you come out like this:

	Splits	Scoops	Losers	Net per Hand
Bet Only	8 @ +$350	6 @ +$900	7 @ -$300	+$290 avg.
Bet & Raise	8 @ +$500	6 @ +$1,400	7 @ -$600	+$390 avg.

Not only were you in the best shape to begin with, but the extra raises went to you! This isolated example was laid out longhand to show you the money dynamics of a three-way pot in Hi/Lo Split. But there are several different three-way scenarios and each will have its own set of numbers. With some, the best hand should raise and with others, it shouldn't. If the low already had an 8 made, for instance, any raises would have just fattened up the low hand's numbers.

While it's helpful to see how the money slides around in a three-way pot as the extra bets go in, you don't have to gyrate through every possible scenario to know what to do. All you really need is the bottom line. So here's the part you need to remember about three-way pots:

1. If you have the best high and the low is not yet made—RAISE.
2. If you have the best high and the low is already made—CALL.
3. If you have the best low and you're at least a 2-to-1 favorite for your half—RAISE.
4. If you have the best low and are less than a 2-to-1 favorite—CALL.

Now what kinds of low hands are a 2-to-1 favorite over another low hand? A made 8-6 vs. a 7 draw or a made 8-5 vs. a 6 draw are both better than 2-to-1 favorites and should raise (your second card needs to be lower than your opponent's draw). In the case of a made low vs. another made low, if you're at least one complete rank smoother than your opponent—such as with a made 7-6 vs. a made 8-6—raise. If it's any closer than that, just call.

Concept #64: Play on the Last Two Streets

6TH STREET: Sixth Street in Stud-8 or Better can be very cruel. Things will sometimes turn so sour they will be downright nauseating. It'll often come up when somebody catches four low cards on board that might reach to a straight or a flush or both. When this happens, sometimes your big pair, or your mediocre low hand, should be given up. Here's an example. Suppose that on 6th Street your two opponents show:

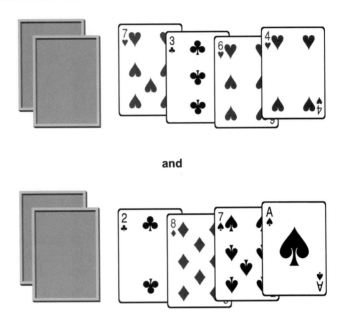

and

If you've still got just a pair of Kings for high and there's a bet, it's probably not worth calling two more bets to see if you'll get a piece of the pot. You were already in jeopardy on 5th Street, but 6th Street just killed you! Unimproved Kings will lose to a straight, a flush, trips, an accidental two small pair and even a pair of Aces. If you already have Kings up, however, you'll just have to bite the bullet and call the hand down—unless the raising begins. Then you might very well have to fold those as well.

Another spot where you can see trouble coming on 6th Street is when the pot's three way and you've got something like a rough 3-7/6-2-8-Q against:

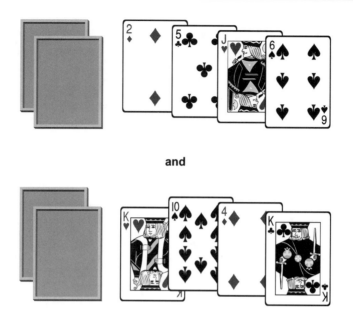

and

Once again, 6th Street blistered you. Nevertheless, the raising is about to commence and you just can't take the heat, so fold before calling that first bet.

7TH STREET: Low hands tend to have a betting advantage over high hands at the river, as they do on most streets. As a result, you can bet more low boards for value against a high board on the end than the other way around. One key example is shown on the following page.

Your opponent came in raising on 3rd Street and kept on betting, but then he checked when it looked as if you made a low on 6th Street. You, in fact, missed your low, but his check on 6th Street indicates he probably still had one big pair at that point. The fact that you both share some of the same cards makes this even more likely. He'll usually check on the end and if you happen to bet, he almost can't raise you even if he's made Kings up. That's because he's practically sure he's only going to split—unless you've made a straight in which case he loses it all. That's why you can bet your two small pair for value in this spot.

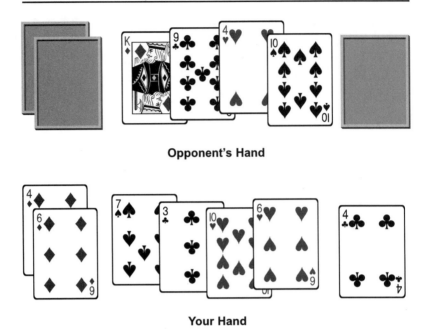

Opponent's Hand

Your Hand

This move frustrates one big pair to no end. He calls, thinking he's probably going to split, then finds out you've rerouted your hand to scoop him. It's true, sometimes you'll bet out with 6s and 4s, get called by two big pair, and feel foolish for having bet. But if you've got reason to believe that he had only one pair on 6th (he checked to you, or his cards looked dead, or both), then he'll still have one pair at the end about 70 percent of the time—but he'll call you nearly 100 percent of the time. You'll make more money on that river bet than you'll lose.

This same principle, that low hands have the betting edge, is true to yet a greater degree when you've made an 8 low with your two little pair. Even if your opponent's board is something like K-2-5-8, he can't possibly have you beaten both ways. If he's backed into a low, the best he can have for high is two Kings. If he's made Kings up, then he can't have a low. Hence, you can bet with complete impunity. Either you'll get back your last bet when you split, or you'll scoop him. Just remember that it takes all seven cards to make two pair (or trips) and a low hand. If just one of the cards is higher than an 8, it can't happen.

Finally, at the river in a three-way pot you very often should not raise when you're an immortal lock for your half because you don't want to drive out an opponent who will realize he's holding a loser. If you make him fold, you can't win another penny.

Here's what I mean. You've got A-2/6-4-8-9/3. You've made a 6-perfect at the river. Your two opponents show:

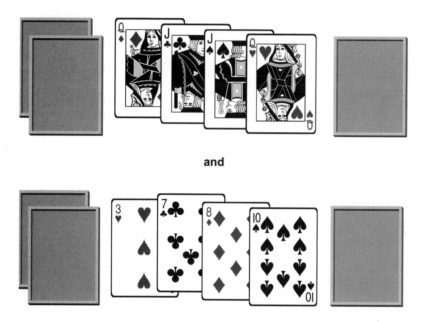

and

and you're positioned in between them. You've got the low locked up since the best possible hand your low opponent could have is a 7. When the open Queens-up bets, you should just call to elicit an overcall from the other low hand. You don't want him to go anywhere!

Note: If your 5th Street card was, say, a 4, pairing your board so that there's some doubt about your having a low, it's probably okay to raise since your low opponent may well call the extra bet even with an 8 low.

Another time you should go ahead and raise with the virtual nuts for low is when your low opponent seems to have a pretty good low hand himself. For example, if he shows something like:

rather than the 3-7-8-10, there's a good chance he'll call both a bet and a raise. So when the high hand bets, go ahead and pop it. You must become familiar with such distinctions and raise only when you're likely to get called or your irresponsible raising will just cost you money in calls that were never made. Of course, if you're last to act in the hand, then by all means raise after the high bets and the low calls, since the "trappee" is already in for one bet and you've got nothing to lose by attempting to add one more. That brings up the next pivotal consideration.

When you're last to act and the high board bets, then the weak low calls, and you raise with your 6-perfect, should the high hand come back over the top and re-raise if he has, say, Queens full? Remember, he wants to make all the money he can with his powerful high. Problem is, if the man in the middle won't call a cold double raise, then that second raise will just drive him out and neither of you will collect another cent.

In situations like this, a good idea of how much punishment the trappee might take can be gotten by noticing just how threatening his direct opponent's board looks. If it's a scary looking sight and the player holding it has just raised, then the Queens full had better meekly call the single raise and be satisfied splitting one fewer bet. Collecting one raise is better than collecting none.

Chapter 8

Omaha Hi/Lo Split (8 or Better)

Omaha Hi/Lo Split-8 or Better is played in just about all public card rooms at all stakes—high, medium and low. It's a game the $4 and $8 players love because of its terrific action, and it's a game the $50/$100 players relish because they can really "screw it down" tight and let the loose action come to them.

Omaha is dealt out of the same format as Texas Hold'em with blinds, a three card flop, etc., etc. The main difference is that each player has four hole cards—of which he must use exactly two. Using exactly two hole cards means if there are four diamonds on the board and you have a diamond in your hand, that's not a flush as it would be in Hold'em! You must have two more diamonds in you're hand! Furthermore, the pot is split between the best high and the best low, providing the low is an 8 or lower. There, too, an Ace-2-3-4 on the board with only a 5 from your hand makes absolutely nothing! You must combine two lows in the hole with three lows on the board to make a low hand. You can, however, interchange your two hole cards any way you see fit to go both ways. Bear in mind also, that a holding like trips in your hand is nearly worthless, since you can only use two hole cards.

Of all the poker forms played in public cards rooms, Omaha makes the biggest hands. That's because nine cards are available to choose from. With four cards in the hole, it's easy to flop a high pair, two pair or a nice low draw. Problem is, it's easy for your opponents too. Where one big pair will usually take down the money in Hold'em and Queens up is often a winner in 7 Stud, it usually takes a straight or a flush to drag the high end of the pot in Omaha. On the low side, an Ace/2 or Ace/3 is normally needed in the hole (coupled with a three-card low board) to capture the low end.

With all those basics out of the way, let's make our first important point about winning at Omaha Hi/Lo Split. That point being—more so than the other three games covered in this book;

Concept #65: Omaha-8 Should Be Played Straight Forward

There are so many cards in this game that most hands which can be made are made. As a result, Omaha-8 is more of a pure card game than a psychological mind game. That means:

1. You won't be able to bluff (or semi-bluff) much.
2. You won't be able to disguise your hand much.

Somebody will often have whatever the board will accommodate. Solid Omaha-8 strategy pretty much boils down to picking a quality starting hand and playing directly according to its relative strength on the flop. The rest will largely take care of itself. So save your fancy, creative maneuvers for Stud and Hold'em. Here are a couple of explicit Omaha-8 situations which illustrate the straightforward nature of the game.

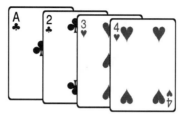

Your Hand

The Flop

Point 1: You're last to act in a four way pot. The first three players have checked and it's up to you. You had a beautiful hand to start out with, but somebody else's flop came up. That's the thing you'll quickly learn about this game. With so many cards in each player's hand, very seldom will everybody miss the flop. If this was Hold'em, you might take a stab at the pot from this position. But in Omaha-8, to even remotely entertain the notion of trying to steal from three players would be a waste of money. Somebody's probably got trip Kings and somebody has a bigger heart flush draw than you. You can almost count on it. As for your "back door" low possibility, it's not worth it. Just take a free card and don't step out of line. Now let's look at another.

Your Hand

The Flop

Point 2: Here's the exact same flop, but this time you've made a monster, Kings full. Problem is, you've got most of the good cards locked up. If you don't bet, nobody's likely to do it for you. No one can have an Ace high flush draw (since you're holding it) and if somebody else has three Kings, they might make a bigger full house than yours later. Besides that, if the next card is a low one you might end up losing that half at the river. So it would be foolish to slowplay here, just bet right out.

These two situations were hand picked, perhaps a little unfairly. But they were meant to show that in Omaha-8 you should usually just bet your good hands and fold your bad ones.

Concept #66: Middle Cards are Poison

You don't have to lose a ton of money at this game to learn this concept. Just look at the three following Omaha-8 starting hands and think about them.

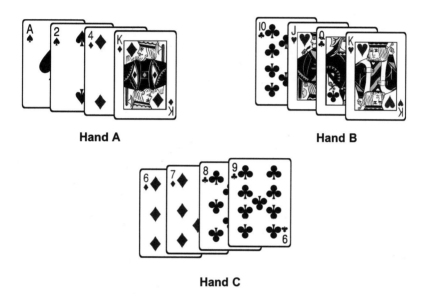

Hand A   **Hand B**

Hand C

Hand A is the most desirable of the three. Not only will it make the "nut" low if three low cards between a 3 and an 8 come up, but the 4 gives it a second shot at low if one of the low board cards is an Ace or a deuce. The suited Ace will make the nut flush if three spades hit the board and the suited King will make a decent flush if the diamonds come. Finally, the Ace/King can make the nut straight if high cards come and might even win with just Aces and Kings.

Hand B isn't a bad holding, either. If high cards flop, it can make a number of straights, flushes and full houses. Yet if low cards come, the hand is easy to get away from.

Now look at hand C. At first glance it may look all right but it's not. If it makes a low, it'll be a bad low. If it makes a flush, it'll probably get beaten by a higher flush. If it makes a straight or flops a set of trips, that almost certainly puts at least one low card on the board that it might lose the other half of the pot to. This hand spells T-R-O-U-B-L-E! In short, middle cards should be avoided like the plague. Take them right out of your starting hand repertoire.

Concept #67: Playable Omaha-8 Starting Hands

Same as with Texas Hold'em, the playability of your starting hand in Omaha depends upon position. The number of players that have come in before you, and whether there's been a raise, tell you a lot about the quality of hole cards you'll be up against. If you're sitting up front, you won't have that kind of information.

No matter how you look at it, though, you want to have either very high or very low cards. Sometimes it's okay to have a couple of each, but better if they're all one or the other. That way you can make more straights and/or good lows. Overall, it's best to have four low cards since four high cards constitute a one way hand.

In the Hold'em section of this book, all 169 possible starting hands were laid out one by one. In Omaha-8, however, there are several thousand. There's no practical way to cover them all. But if there's one chief characteristic that can make an Omaha Hi/Lo hand valuable, it's having an Ace/deuce in it. That will make you a front-runner for the low half. If you've got another "wheel" card with your Ace/deuce (a 3, 4, or 5), so much the better in case the Ace or the deuce gets "counterfeited" (duplicated) on board. And if your Ace is suited so that you might make a nut flush, better still. The more ways your four cards can work together to mesh with a lot of flops, the more potential it has. The illustration below is the epitome of a dream Omaha Hi/Lo hand:

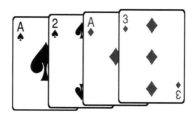

This has everything described in the preceding paragraph, and more. The fourth card is also a suited Ace. So with this hand you could make three different wheels (if part of the board contained A/4/5, 2/4/5, or 3/4/5), two nut flushes (spades or diamonds), a set of Aces (if an Ace hits the board) or Aces full (if an Ace and a pair hit).

That's the kind of power and versatility you'd love to have in an Omaha-8 hand. It's a true first-class start. Other first class starters are cited below:

A/2/3/4
A/2/3/any
A/A/2/any
A/3/4/K with suited Ace
A/A/K/K with suited Ace

Every hand shown here has a number of ways to win the money. An A/2/3/4 is almost sure to make the nut low if three low cards come (a low will be possible about 60 percent of the time at the end of the hand). A suited Ace would make the hand even better.

A/2/3/any has enough ways to make the nut low that it's playable on the merits of that alone—and the more suited it may be, the better.

A/A/2/any combines "the thing" (Ace/deuce) for low with top pair going in. That makes it playable from any seat.

A/3/4/K isn't as good as the first three hands, but three wheel cards plus a suited Ace makes it a legitimate premium start.

A/A/K/K is not as versatile since it's a one way hand, but has lots of ways to make a big set, a big flush or a full house. The weak aspect of this—and all high hands—is that they almost need to flop two high cards to remain potentially strong. The problem is that *a low draw or a made low will come on the flop two times out of three.*

Still, there are very few starting hands in this game, high or low that are worth a true value raise before the flop, since Omaha is quite a "draw out" game. The main benefit of pre-flop raises is that they can drive players out, giving you position on those in front of you. Nonetheless, any time you pick up one of the five hands described above (or something very similar to them) you can come in raising right from an early seat. Now for a look at some second string playable hands:

2/3/4/5
A/3/Q/Q
A/2/any/any
A/K/Q/J
K/K/Q/Q

2/3/4/5 has all its cards nicely interlaced. Its disadvantage is that you almost need an Ace to flop or you've got a trouble hand. Still, it's a quality holding.

A/3 with a Big Pair is also usually worth a look. Its down side is that you can hit a pretty good flop and not have or be drawing to the nuts.

A "naked" Ace/deuce (with nothing else of particular value) is such a key component that it alone is usually worth seeing the flop with. It would be a little nicer, though, if your other two cards ran in sequence, such as with A/2/6/7 or A/2/10/J, or if the Ace was suited.

A/K/Q/J is a one-way hand that you'll either love or hate on the flop. A suited Ace would give it some extra value.

Two big pair in your hand aren't bad, but they're nothing to get wild about. If you don't flop a straight draw or a set of trips, you'll probably be mucking them right there.

When, where and how do you play these second-string hands? Up front, they're just worth a call—and only if it's not a "shoot 'em up" game in which it's usually raised and often re-raised before the flop. If it is, you should probably pass them from an early seat, but call from middle position or later. If you have one of these in the last three seats and it hasn't been raised yet, pop it yourself unless there are already lots of flat callers. In a multi-way pot, just limp in quietly. Now, for a few sometimes playable third string hands:

3/4/5/6
8/9/10/J
A/4/Q/J
A/4/10/10
2/3/4/K

3/4/5/6 is a nice flowing hand, but it's only very good when both an Ace and a deuce hit the board. Other than that, it's apt to make a lot of losing straights. Beware!

8/9/10/J can be a nice hand when two high cards flop. But you can get blistered if the board is something like 7/10/J/4/Q or 5/J/Q/4/K (a bigger straight will likely beat you).

A/4/Q/J could make some winning highs and some winning lows, but you won't find yourself drawing to the nuts very often—this requires delicate management.

A/4/10/10 is a similar story as the preceding hand. You need to play well to stay out of trouble with it.

2/3/4/K has three wheel cards, but no Ace. It's forte is when an Ace with one or two other low cards flop. With this type of hand it's pretty much this: no Ace on the flop—no play.

With the last three holdings and others like them, it would be a considerable help if the Ace or King were suited. Either way, all five are examples of marginal Omaha-8 hands.

You'd basically throw them away anywhere in the first six seats. If there's been no raise, just limp in with them in the last three or four seats—unless you're the first one in. Then raise it in an attempt to get heads-up with the blinds.

Note on Blind Play: What if you're the small blind in an unraised pot? Then it's okay to pay the half bet and see the flop with a lot of mediocre to weak hands that haven't even been mentioned because no single starting Omaha hand is really all that much better than any other.

In Hold'em, for example, pocket Aces are a 7-to-1 favorite over a 2/7 offsuit. But A/A/K/K unsuited in Omaha is only 2-to-1 to get the high end over a rag hand like 2/7/9/Q unsuited. The down side of playing from the blind is that you'll be out of position the whole way. So if there's been no raise and the big blind isn't the type who often raises from that position, go ahead and call from the small blind with about the top half of all your hands. This might include holdings as weak as 2/4/6/Q and 2/4/J/J. But be careful not to trap yourself with them on the flop.

Playing from the big blind is more cut and dried. Either you can come in for free or have to pay a full bet or more. To call a raise out of position, you need a good hand, second-string minimum such as the likes of A/2/any/any or 2/3/4/5.

Concept #68: You've Got Nothing 'Till the Flop

In nearly all other poker games, you can have a darn good hand right on the initial deal. Not so in Omaha Hi/Lo. An unimproved pair of Aces or Kings will take down the money once in a blue moon, but in general until the dealer puts up the flop, you've got nothing.

Because of this, many players feel they have to get in there and see which three cards will hit the board. This isn't right. If you divide the price of your blinds by the nine hands you'll receive per round, each hand will cost a mere one sixth of a small bet. At $30/$60 stakes for example, a $15 small blind plus a $30 big blind will average out to a cost of $5 per hand. Folding and giving up that prorated $5 is a lot cheaper than calling for $30 (or $60 in a raised pot) with questionable cards just because an A/3/5 could flop to your 2/4/6/8. What's more likely is that you'll flop a couple of "sucker draws" that will just get you into trouble. So save your money until you've either got a premium hand, or are in one of the blinds and can get in for a half bet or less.

On the Flop: Even when the flop fits your hand pretty well, you very often have just an assortment of good draws rather than a made hand. This is where the premium hands excel. They'll flop the nuts, or draws to the nuts, more often than non-premium hands. Here's an example of two hands, one premium, the other mediocre and how they compare to each other.

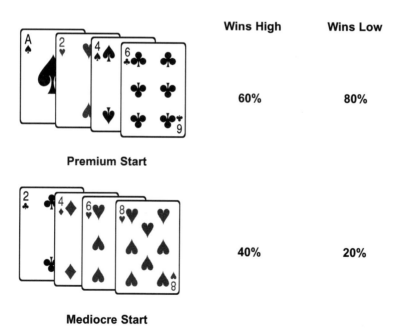

Wins High   Wins Low

60%   80%

Premium Start

40%   20%

Mediocre Start

If these two hands were in the pot together heads up, the premium hand would be a 3-to-2 favorite for the high and a 4-to-1 favorite to get the low (when there is a low). Now suppose the following typical flop comes down:

The premium start has flopped a nut-low draw (needing an A, 2, 4, 5, 6 or 8), a gut-shot straight draw (needing a 5), a back-door wheel draw (needing an A/5, 2/5 or 4/5) and a back-door nut-flush draw (needing any two spades).

The mediocre start by comparison has the third or fourth best low draw (needing a 2, 4, 5, 6 or 8) with a gut shot at the nut low (needing an Ace), a gut-shot straight draw (needing a 5) and a back door draw at a weak flush (needing any two hearts).

Both players could look at this flop and say to themselves, "Well, I've got this draw, that draw and the other draw, so I've gotta play." From this vantage point, though, we can see that the premium start has several ways to make hands that will most likely win—while the mediocre start has several ways to make hands that have a much greater chance of getting beat. That's what you need to look out for. If you've flopped a draw instead of a made hand make sure your draw is to the nuts so that it will win if it gets there. This is particularly true with low draws, since somebody often has the nut low at the river. Draws to the current nuts for high, however, are almost always at risk. The nut flush for example will often get knocked off by a full house if the board pairs, but worse yet, a lower flush may never have been the best hand at any time.

Concept #69: Multi-Plex Straight Draws

With four cards in your hand and three on the flop, there can be several ways that you might make a straight with two more cards to still to come. These "multi-plex" straight draws tend to dominate the play of the hand in Omaha and you should be aware of them. Here's a good example:

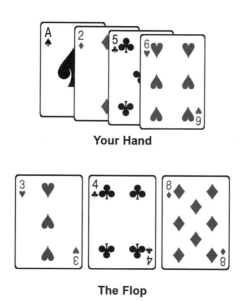

Your Hand

The Flop

You already have the nuts for low, but any Ace, deuce, 5, 6, or 7 will give you a straight. That's two shots at 16 cards, making you a 3-to-2 favorite to get there. Be aware, however, that there are really only three cards you truly want, the Ace, deuce or 7. The 5 or 6, while preserving your nut low, are liable to just make somebody else a higher straight, costing you half the pot or possibly more. These dilemmas are not uncommon. Here's what happens when each of your possible straight cards come to your A/2/5/6:

Final Board Is	You Have	The Nut High Is
3-4-8-K-A	Wheel	Wheel
3-4-8-K-2	Wheel & 6 Hi Straight	6 Hi Straight
3-4-8-K-7	Nut Low & 7 Hi Straight	7 Hi Straight
3-4-8-K-5	Wheel & 6 Hi Straight	8 Hi Straight
3-4-8-K-6	Nut Low & 6 Hi Straight	8 Hi Straight

When the 5 or the 6 comes, making an 8-high straight possible, somebody won't always have it, but they will *often* have it. Typical examples would be when an opponent holds A/2/5/7, A/3/5/7, A/4/5/7 or A/5/6/7 and the 6 comes. Against his last three holdings, you still get your low half of the pot. But against the first one, he gets the high and you'll split the low with him, and you'll have been "quartered." So actually, you have 16 outs to make your straight, but only 10 outs to the nuts.

Understanding the difference between "outs to your hand" and "outs to the nuts" carries much more weight when you've got a one way hand, such as the one shown on the following page.

This time you don't have much of a hand just yet (a pair of Jacks), but several good draws. Any 9, Queen, King, or Ace will make you the nut straight. Furthermore, any straight card except the Ace will lock out all the low draws. That makes it look like you've got two tries at 13 cards which is an even-money shot—and most of them for the whole pot! Well, if nobody had a set of trips, two pair or spades, that would be true. But that's not how it usually works in Omaha.

The reality is that four of your straight cards (the Ace, King, Queen, and 9 of spades) will most likely give somebody else a flush. Besides that, if the board pairs you'll probably lose to a full house. So how often will you make your straight and still end up with the nuts for high? The following breakdown tells you the odds of what will happen if you have this kind of hand 25 times:

Your Hand

The Flop

Pair or spade comes on the turn   **Fold 10 times**

Blank on the turn (no straight, spade or pair) 10 times:
Miss at the river   Fold seven times
Make straight at river w/ a spade   Fold one time
Make straight at river w/clean board   **Win two times**

Make straight on the turn w/clean board 5 times:
Board pairs at the river   Fold one time
Spade comes at the river   Fold one time
Straight remains the nuts   **Win three times**

Even though you were a 50-50 shot on the flop to make the nut straight, that would be the nuts at the river only five times in 25. Assuming that you fold if the turn card is a pair or a spade (and you should unless it's a Jack), you'll finish up with the nuts about one third of all the times you come past the turn. If you're a good player, you might be able to sense it when you've got your straight made and the river pairs or a spade comes—yet your hand is still good. But it's usually not worth calling on the end just as a matter of principle. And whatever you do, never call a bet on the turn still looking to make your straight—when the three flush cards or the pair are out there on the board.

Concept #70: Drawing to the Nut Low

When you start out with your basic Acey/deucey in the hand, how often will you win the low half of the pot? Let's say you have A/2/J/J and the flop comes down:

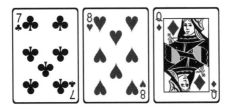

All you need is any 3, 4, 5, or 6 on the turn or the river (providing the other card isn't an Ace or a deuce, thereby "counterfeiting" you) and you've got the nuts for low. In this situation, you're just about dead even money to get there.

Now, what if you held a third, good, low card such as A/2/3/X? Then if an Ace or a deuce comes up, you've still got two live cards and will again have the nut low. Ahh, but what if an Ace comes on the turn *and* a deuce pops at the river? In that case, you'll need a fourth low card such as with A/2/3/4 to still make the nuts. The chart below lists the odds to make your low when either one or two low cards flop, depending upon how many low cards you have in your hand.

You Hold	Flop Is	Odds to Make Any Low	Odds to Make The Nuts
1. A/2/J/J	7-8-Q	1.5-to-1 favorite	even money
2. A/2/3/J	7-8-Q	2.5-to-1 favorite	2-to-1 favorite
3. A/2/3/4	7-8-Q	2.5-to-1 favorite	2.5-to-1 favorite
4. A/2/6/J	7-8-Q	2.5-to-1 favorite	8-to-7 underdog
5. A/2/J/J	8-Q-K	5-to-1 underdog	5-to-1 underdog
6. A/2/3/J	8-Q-K	3-to-1 underdog	3-to-1 underdog
7. A/2/3/4	8-Q-K	3-to-1 underdog	3-to-1 underdog
8. A/2/6/J	8-Q-K	3-to-1 underdog	6-to-1 underdog

The odds in the previous table have been rounded off slightly just to give you a good basic feel for where you stand with certain low draws and certain flops. That's all fine, but just knowing those odds doesn't tell you how to play the hand. The number of players in the pot and whether it's been raised, or is likely to be raised, will all affect the situation. Here's some math-generated strategy for each case.

Case #1: A/2/hi/hi with two lows on board: This is a common dilemma which comes up much more often than the other seven. If you have basically no outs on the high side, and it's just a three-way pot in which there was no raise (even a single raise) or before the flop, don't call to the river trying to make your low. The times you miss, combined with the times you get there and are "quartered" with another nut low, tend to make this play a loser. Instead, just call the smaller bet on the flop if you're in last position and it hasn't been raised, or are pretty sure it won't get raised behind you. But if you miss on the turn, give it up. In a three-way pot, the only way you'd ever call on the turn would be if it was double-raised before the flop (increasing your pot odds) and you can see the river card for one bet.

Now, if the pot is at least four-way, and you can get in for one bet on the flop, call. If you miss on the turn and can again get in for one bet, call to the river. Do not call on the flop or the turn if it's been raised or if it looks as if it may well get raised, unless this pot was double-raised before the flop. Then play the hand all the way out.

Case #2 or #3: A/2/3/hi or A/2/3/4 with two lows on board: In these situations you should almost always play. Not only will you make the nut low much more often, but plenty of times you'll get there with an Ace or a deuce, counterfeiting one of your low opponents. Hence, you'll get quartered less often when you make your hand. About the only times you should fold these hands are when there's been no raise before the flop, the jamming (raising) has begun and you feel everybody's got a low along their other outs. Then you might get "sixthed" (have to split the low three ways giving you one sixth of the pot).

Case #4: A/2/6/hi with two lows on board: Having a third low card in your hand that is not a "nut" card gives you just as many ways to make a low as if you held A/2/3—but many of them will just be an "emergency low." If an Ace popped, for example, you'd have the seventh best low with your 2/6. Besides that, with a third low card, it's just a shade tougher to make the nut low since that 6 in your hand is one fewer card that could hit the board and do it for you. The closer to a 3 your third low card is, of course, the better your low will be if you have to use it (your third card). So the smoother your third low card, the more you should play similarly to Case #2. The rougher it is, the closer to Case #1 your strategy should be.

Case #5: A/2/hi/hi with one low on board: Without some considerable high potential, this hand should virtually always be thrown away. It's very hard to make money getting half the pot one time in six. There's just one remote spot in which you might try. The pot must be at least four way, it must have been raised before the flop and you must be able to see the turn card for one small bet, plus have legitimate suspicions that there might not be a bet on 4th Street. If, however, you've come to the turn, have picked up the low draw and, to your dismay, there is a bet, you must call.

Case #6 or #7: A/2/3/hi or A/2/3/4 with one low on board: As nice as your hand is, you still need to hit two running low cards. There's no way you can get enough payback from a three-way pot, so regardless of the situation, three-way pots are out. In any four-way pot, however, you can call along as long as you don't have to pay a raise. These include pots that were not raised before the flop. But as soon as there's a raise, or if it looks like there's going to be one, release it, unless there was a pre-flop raise and you've picked up a nut low draw which can't be counterfeited.

Case #8: A/2/6/hi with one low on board: If your third low card really is a 6, then you should play your hand just about the same as Case #5. But if it were a 4, using that when you have to, will generally give you the second nut low, and occasionally the stone nuts. In that case you can play in four-way pots if they were raised before the flop and not raised on the flop. But never call a raise on the turn, unless the turn card was a 3 specifically.

Summary: Note that all recommendations concerning low draws were made on the strength of the low only. Any reasonable high "outs" you may have should "loosen you up" in proportion to their potential.

Concept #71: Getting Counterfeited

Okay, so you've got an A/2/K/K in a four way pot and the flop comes down:

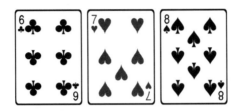

You can almost certainly kiss the high half of the pot good-bye, but you've flopped the nut low. However, with all those players in, you're worried that maybe somebody has the Ace/deuce with you. Well, that's only half your worries! Why? Because one time out of four in this spot, you'll get counterfeited!

Being counterfeited means a card hits the board that wrecks your low. And with two cards to come, an Ace or a deuce will fall 25 percent of the time. That's the nightmare of already having the nut low with no backup card such as a 3 or a 4.

If you were already at 4th Street with a "naked" nut low leaving only one card to come, your hand would be more likely to stand up. Also, if you held four live nut-low cards on the flop (such as A/2/3/4 with the above flop) or three of them on the turn (A/2/3), your hand would then actually be "counterfeit-proof." The following chart tells how often your nut low will get counterfeited from various points in the hand to the river—with and without backup nut low cards.

Your Hand	The Flop	You'll Get Counterfeited	The Turn	You'll Get Counterfeited
A/2/K/K	6-7-8	1 out of 4	6-7-8-9	1 out of 7
A/2/3/K	6-7-8	1 out of 36	6-7-8-9	Never
A/2/3/4	6-7-8	Never	6-7-8-9	Never

So what does it all mean? It means that in five out of six situations, the prospect of getting counterfeited is not a major threat and shouldn't affect your strategy. But that sixth situation can be a haunting predicament. That's the one where you have the nut low on the flop with no backup cards

(A/2/K/K). Between getting counterfeited a fourth of the time, and maybe being quartered if your hand stands up, your potential return is much weaker than it would seem. This hand is at its most vulnerable when there are lots of players in and everybody seems to be raising. That usually tells you one or two other players have the nut low with you, but they have high strength as well. It's almost unthinkable to consider throwing away the nuts, but if they are going to keep pounding the pot, it just might be best to get out.

You'd need a pretty severe scenario to make this correct, so I'll describe one. Suppose you have the hand pictured at the introduction to this concept in that four-way pot and the stakes are $50/$100. The 6-7-8 flops and somebody bets. There's a raise and a re-raise, then it comes to you. If you're going to have to call $150 here, maybe $200 on the turn and, say, another $100 at the river you'll have $450 in at the showdown (from this point going forward). If everybody goes all the way, there will be about $2,100 in the final pot counting the blinds and all. Now, understand that your chances of getting half in this particular pot are practically nil. What you'll probably get back is either a quarter ($525), or maybe a sixth ($350). But that's not all! What about that 25 percent of the time when you get counterfeited and end up with nothing?

Want to see things a little clearer? Just picture yourself having this hand four times, getting back $525 twice (quartered), $350 once (sixthed), and nothing that fourth time when you've been counterfeited. It's true, when you get counterfeited you don't pay off the last bet (and maybe not the turn bets either if that's where your hand went bad). Still, you'd have invested around $1,600 on all four hands combined and gotten back only $1,400—less if you get sixthed a couple of times. You can plug in your own different betting scenarios and see how you come out. This is where you're going to have to use some good poker sense. If your opponents in this hand are the types who'll jam it up only with the nuts and/or superior two-way hands, you should probably release your vulnerable nut low early and sit this one out. On the other hand, if they fire chips in the pot rather irresponsibly, fasten your seat belt and go along for the ride.

As for the other five nut-low situations described in the preceding chart, you'll just have to play them out—and if you get counterfeited, you get counterfeited.

Concept #72: Quartered at the River

Many times you'll get to the river and have the nuts for low with the customary Ace/deuce in your hand. What's wrong with that? Well, when the board is something like:

it's not too unlikely that you'll be splitting your low half with somebody else, since most people will always play any kind of Ace/deuce hand. Because of that, when you've got the typical Acey/deucey nut low at the river, it's important how many players are in the pot.

If it's just three-way action, you generally shouldn't raise. The reason is that the good high hand will force the betting, being pretty sure of winning half. But if you end up getting quartered (getting half of the low half), you'll lose money on every new bet you put in (if three of you put in $100 apiece at the river, the high hand will get back $150 and the two lows will get back $75 each).

If it was a four-way pot when you got quartered, you'd break even on all river bets while getting half would earn you a dollar for a dollar. But even then you can't raise with complete impunity because some four-way pots will have three Ace/deuce nut lows. Then you'll end up with one third of the low half, or a sixth of the pot. In that case every extra $100 you've put in will have cost you $33 net, even though the pot is four-way. So you can see that raising at the river with the nut low is risky business, mostly when the nuts are an Ace/deuce and to a lesser extent when the nuts are Ace/3.

Does that mean you should never raise on the end with the nut low? Not quite. By paying attention you'll sometimes be able to gain a feel for which way your opponents are going. Then you'll be able to call, saving money when you're getting quartered—and raise, making a little extra when you're alone with the low half. Look at the following board:

The pot is just three way. You've got A/2/Q/K with the Ace/Q of hearts. You flopped a "13 out" nut-straight draw and a back-door nut-flush draw, but ended up at the river with the nut low. There's a bet and a call, then you're next. Thinking back, you remember that the pot was bet and raised on the flop by your two opponents. Yes, it is possible that either of them might have the Ace/deuce with you, but it was high hands that they were pushing earlier since the flop contained primarily high cards. Now, the nut low comes at the river along with the original club-flush draw, plus a low straight—and there's a bet followed by a slow call. Since your hand came in "backwards" and the caller in the middle appeared tentative, it's more likely they have high hands and you can probably raise.

If you're wrong and get quartered, you'll lose $25 on a $100 raise; but if you're right and get half, your raise will win an extra $50. The way this hand developed, it's probably worth gambling the extra bet.

Caution: Don't assume that raising in a three-way pot breaks out even if you get quartered two times out of three (since you either win $50 or lose $25). That's not necessarily so. What if the original bettor has the nut high, re-raises and you get quartered? Now your raise combined with his will cost you $50.

Often the nut high will re-raise and, if the man in the middle has a loser, he'll usually see the light and fold, earning you nothing extra at all. But if the middle player has the nut low with you, he'll call all bets and you'll both lose money on the extra action. Hence, if you are quartered, there may be a couple of raises to reckon with; and if you're not quartered, there might not be any caller in the middle to pay you off. So, before raising with the nut low in a three way pot, you ought to have a decent feel for two things:

1. Whether the man in the middle has a non-nut hand (be it high or low)—or the nut low with you.
2. Whether the original bettor (who's likely got the nut high) has the "poise" to not re-raise a non-nut hand out of the pot.

If he's going to put in maximum raises simply because he's got the nuts, then your own raise can only cost you money because either the middleman folds a loser, making you nothing, or you get quartered, losing $50. With all that being said, there's still one other time you can usually raise at the river with just the nut low in a three-way pot. That's when the nuts is an unlikely holding, such as with the board pictured on the following page:

Final Board

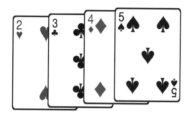

Your Hand

Here, your 3/4 is the nuts for low and most of those will have been thrown in the muck before the flop. So a raise in this spot will probably earn you $50 rather than cost you $25 or $50.

Four-Way Pots: When you raise at the river with the nut low in a four-way pot, a whole bunch of times you'll just get your money back (when you get quartered), sometimes you'll win even money (when you get half), and occasionally you'll lose 33 percent (when you get sixthed). Be aware here that the original bettor could have the nut high plus the nut low, and you'll get sixthed with him and another nut low. In these cases, he'll nearly always re-raise because he knows he's getting two-thirds of the pot—minimum.

Nevertheless, you'd have to get sixthed three times for every two times you got half to not make any money by raising. Because of that, it's usually worth going through the exercise of putting in the raise. Still though, there's no substitute for being able to read where you are in the hand and whether the original bettor will only re-raise, knocking out a high hand who would have called one raise, but not two.

Chapter 9

Things You Can't Read in a Book

Lots of professional poker players learned everything they know from the school of hard knocks. These particular guys couldn't tell you the odds of making a flush with two cards to come if their lives depended upon it. Yet, they'll virtually never make the wrong play when faced with that situation. If a flush will win and their hand is live, they'll draw to it. If there's a prominent chance they'll make the flush and lose, their hand hits the muck right now.

I know players like this. They're "street players." Since they were "poker babies," they honed their poker skills by absorbing and digesting everything they've ever seen happen at the poker table. When you're thinking during a hand, they're tapping into your brain—feeling and interpreting every flinch.

When one of these players heard I was writing a book on poker he said to me, "Freddie, do you really think you can teach people to win at poker by writing about pot odds and outs and all that crap? I mean that's good and all, but there are some things you gotta just know—just feel, that you can't read in a book."

He's right. He wasn't talking about sorcery or ESP. What my friend was referring to was the super subtleties that slip right past most recreational poker players. They're a combination of minute hints, barely noticeable that give you precious insight into what's happening in this particular hand—right now. This goes beyond poker odds—beyond the textbook. Reading and pouring over poker literature can make you a formidable opponent. But you can never become a lethal poker player until you develop this extra sense.

So for you poker players out there who weren't blessed with an astute poker "street sense" at birth, here are just a few of those all important—things you can't read in a book!

Concept #73: What's Happening This Time Around?

Did you know that the odds against being dealt a roll up (trips on the first three cards) in 7 Stud are 424-to-1. I often go for days and days without being rolled up. But odds are just odds and only tell you what you can expect with no other information. Every time you play a hand of poker, however, you're gathering and processing valuable information. The reason you do that is so you can draw conclusions which are more accurate than just going by blind odds. In that sense, playing by the odds is a fallback—something you're forced to resort to when you don't have anything better to go on. But winning poker players nearly always have more to go on than just the odds. Look at the following 7 Stud hand illustration:

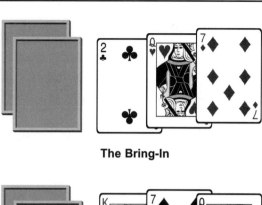

The Bring-In

The Initial Raiser

Your Hand

The deuce of clubs brought it in, the King raised, then both you and the deuce called. You're curious as to what the deuce might have called a raise with, since he's a pretty snug player. Right now you think he might have clubs, maybe deuces with an Ace kicker, or he might even be slowplaying buried Aces. On the turn the King bet, you called and the deuce called along also. With three clubs now in your own hand and the deuce not turning aggressive with a raise, he no longer seems to have clubs or buried Aces – probably just the deuces with an Ace kicker. On 5th Street, the King bet again, you raised with your Queens up and now the deuce re-raises! What's his hand? Forget about 424-to-1. He's rolled up! Finally, it all fits into place.

This scenario was concocted with nearly perfect cards to boldly illustrate that sometimes it doesn't matter what the odds are. The play will reveal that this opponent just has to have a particular hand, regardless. If you still want to look at it mathematically, you might ask yourself this question; "Of all the times a tight deuce calls a raise on 3rd Street against two picture cards, then calls on the turn with an offsuit deuce/Queen, then re-raises on 5th Street with most of his 7s and Queens dead, what percentage of those times will he be rolled up? The answer is, virtually all of them! This, right now, is that one time in 425.

Usually a player's hand won't be that obvious, but signs will always be there. What are his exposed cards (in stud games)? What position did he do that from (in flop games)? Was the pot raised earlier? Is he a tight or loose player? Does he just bet his hands, or is he a cagey bettor? Is he on his game, or stuck and steaming? You've got to pick up on those signs and develop your reads and then learn to trust them!

It's fine to know that having pocket Aces in Hold'em is a 220-to-1 shot, or that flopping a set with a pocket pair is 7-to-1 against. But that alone won't do you any good if you can't figure out ahead of time that in this hand, right here, right now, your pocket Aces are no good. Any poker mope can just play his own cards. Winners must figure out what's happening this particular time around. That's what you need to focus on.

Concept #74: Respect Your Superiors; Intimidate Your Inferiors

Unless you're a world champion, you probably won't be the best player at the table each and every time you sit down to play poker. There will be people who can outplay you and people you can outplay. Remember that, theoretically, the deck is supposed to break even over your lifetime. At least, that's the only reasonable assumption to make when you play. Your game plan, however, is to turn a net lifetime profit with merely average cards, an interesting challenge. There are three basic ways to do that and you'll probably have to learn them all. They are:

1. Save bets with your losing hands.
2. Earn extra bets with your winning hands.
3. Win an occasional pot that your cards couldn't do on their own.

Number 1 is just good basic poker. The earlier you can read when you're beat and aren't getting the pot odds to chase, the better off your bankroll will be. You must strive to save bets against all levels of opponents, be they tough or soft.

Numbers 2 and 3 are more delicate challenges. This is where your poker strategy should diverge a bit. At every table you should objectively evaluate where you rank along the poker food chain. That is, who are you going to make your money from, and who do you merely not want to lose any to? If you're in a pot against somebody whose ability you totally respect, in fact admire, he's probably the better player. Trying to save bets against him may not be that tough. But attempting to trap him for extra bets, or "leverage" him out of the pot isn't likely to work because he'll probably see through

your play. Don't make the right play against the wrong player.

That's an important distinction to make. For this reason, you should save your fancier moves for players you feel
you can maneuver. It's against them that you should try to
earn an extra bet with a check/raise or by giving a free card,
etc. It is they that you might attempt to intimidate into folding if you're in good position, suspect they're weak or have a
scary board. In short, only try to outplay players you can outplay.

As for your superiors, play them more honest. Take
better starting hands up against them because you might be
giving up a little in the play of the hand. That will be the only
edge you'll ever have on them, that is, until you become the
better player.

You know how there are some players who you feel
like you're sitting above and can just tell where they're at?
Well, that's how you look to some others. You should spend
most of your time in pots with players you know how to handle. The toughies? Study them intently from the sidelines
every pot they're in and learn. That's how you move up the
food chain.

Concept #75: The Better You Get, the Looser You Can Play

You'll go through many phases of playing styles as the caliber
of your own poker game evolves. As rookies, most players are
far too loose. What they do is lose lots of money, then learn
some solid fundamentals and become tight rocks. But that's
probably the best place for a poker player to start out anyway,
as a tight rock. You stay away from all the hands that have an
insidious way of just costing you money.

From there, little by little, you learn to expand your
playing horizons. You acquire the poker sense to take more

marginal hands, turn a modest profit with them if it's possible and get away from them when it's not likely to work out. By the time you're a journeyman, you're making money with hands that were losers for you before.

They don't play 5 Card Draw in most public card rooms today, but the most vivid and concise example of this basic principle that I can think of comes from Draw Poker, so here it is. You're playing some eight-handed Jacks or Better and are dealt:

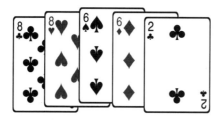

in the #2 seat. The first player checks and it's up to you. In the days when you were a rookie you would have opened it right up. What the heck, two pair is plenty better than a pair of Jacks. It's a playing hand! But since you've come of age you've learned that two little pair in Draw Poker must be played against just one player, *or not at all.* So you check. Now you watch closely as the action moves around the table. When it gets back to you if it's been opened and called, that's too many players. You've got to fold this marginal hand. But if it's just the opener only, now's the time to raise!

You do this (raise) for two reasons. First, to get more money in with what's probably the best hand. Second, to dissuade other players from calling with one pair higher than 8s. It's not that hard to improve one pair on the draw. Improving two pair is like pulling teeth. So you can't afford multiple players all drawing to one pair against you. That mistake is for rookies.

The point of that Draw Poker scenario is, if you play two small pair only in the right situations, you'll make money with them on average. But if you insist on playing every time you get them, you'd be better off if you just threw them all away. There are several less obvious analogies in every poker form, but the principle is the same: If you know in which spots to play marginal hands, they'll make you money. If you can't tell the difference, you should just tighten up and *never* play them.

An example from 7 Card Stud might be a 4/5/6 on your first three cards. Another case from Texas Hold'em could occur when the flop comes 10-7-5 to your pocket 8s. A good Omaha-8 example might be when the flop is 2-6-8 and you've got A/4 with nothing else. And in Stud-8 or Better, it could be that 5-7/7 on 3rd Street. All these hands would require the poker sense to dodge bullets. Without the savvy, just chuck them all. Learn your limitations and play within them!

Concept #76: When a Player Suddenly Bets

Every once in a while during a hand, a player will make a surprise move out of the blue that you didn't expect. Here's what I mean. Let's say you're in a Stud hand and came in raising with a pair of split Jacks. Two players call you to 5th Street where the board now looks like this:

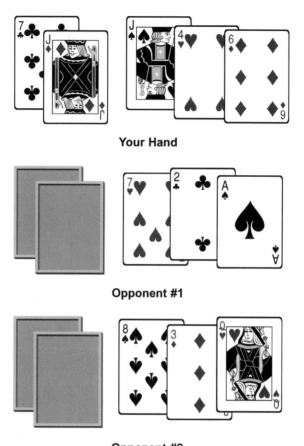

Your Hand

Opponent #1

Opponent #2

The Ace has fallen high on board, but he checks. You're planning to bet when it gets to you—when suddenly the Queen bets in front of you! Well you know what? *The Queen paired him!*

That may seem too simple, but if the card doesn't fit into any straight or flush schemes, a straight forward player will have paired that Queen in a high majority of cases! You're probably against Queens up. Release it and save two or three top bets! Then watch intently as the hole cards are turned over at the river. You won't be wrong very often.

These kinds of tip-offs can come in various forms. You might be heads up in the hand all the way to 6th Street where your lone opponent makes:

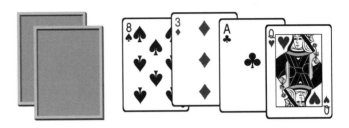

If he checked and called when he caught the Ace on 5th Street, then bet when he caught the Queen on 6th Street—he most likely paired the Queen or already had you beat! His reason for not trying to check/raise would be that you might not bet, now that two overcards have fallen. About the only way you'd still have the best hand here would be if he's thinking at a level where he's actually hoping you'll throw your hand away. A shrewd player might do that if he has say, buried 9s. That'll be up to you to judge—but if you never believe, you'll never make a good laydown.

Concept #77: How's Your Opponent Doing?

The majority of poker players are more conservative and think more clearly when they're winning than when they're losing. Sometimes a certain scenario shapes up during a poker hand that indicates you're beat and should give up your hand. Yet at other times those same signs from the same player shouldn't be taken as seriously. Look at the following Hold'em hand:

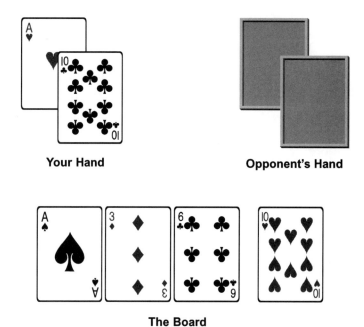

Your Hand   **Opponent's Hand**

The Board

There was no raise before the flop. You checked when the A/3/6 flopped and your opponent bet—then you called. When the 10 fell on the turn to make you Aces up you checked again. Your opponent bet again, then you check-raised and he re-raised. Normally, his re-raise after having been check-raised at this late stage of the hand would be such an aggressive move that he'd almost have to have a set of 3s or 6s and you should probably fold. If your opponent is thinking straight, he realizes that either the 10 helped you big time or you were laying a trap all along, yet he came back over the top with another raise.

But wait! How's your opponent doing in the game at the moment? Suppose it's a $20/$40 game and he's stuck $2000. Is he the type of player who flips a little open at these times? If so, he might only be thinking about the quality of his own hand, and wants to get back all the money he can as fast as he can. He may no longer be thinking rationally enough to realize that your check-raise means you've got a pretty strong hand yourself. His reasoning may be shorted out. In this spot, he might only have A/K or an A/3 or A/6 and you should call.

This is an example of how you should not only play the player, but also play that player's *mood* at the time. There are some solid players who behave nearly the same whether they're way out in front or stuck like a pig—but these are few. The more gamble a poker player has in him, the more that tendency to gamble comes out when he's losing. So when it suddenly looks like you've become the "trappee" instead of the trapper, stop and take note of your opponent's playing style and whether he's winning or losing. If he gambles just to gamble and he's really stuck, you're going to have to call him down when you would normally appear to have the worst of it.

Epilogue

Keep in mind that every morsel of poker strategy presented in this book is subject to variation, debate and even possible amendment. That's because poker is a very inexact science depending upon a multitude of psychological variables.

If this were a blackjack book, I could tell you to always hit 12 against a dealer's 7, no matter what—and there could be no argument. But in poker, whether to raise at the river with Queens up in 7 Stud depends largely upon your opponent. Would he have bet with less than Queens up in the first place? Will he call with less than Queens up if you do raise? Might a raise even get him to fold a hand better than Queens up? This is what makes poker the infinitely deep game that it is. That's why several world class pros can argue to no end over how a specific hand should be played in a certain situation. The basic odds are always there, but everything else depends upon the players. It's also why no poker manual can ever serve as the "be all—end all" of poker strategy.

Still, if you're anything less than a professional poker player right now, learning all the principles in this text will improve your game appreciably. It will get you thinking along the right lines. As you groom your play to expert levels, you'll begin to recognize on your own when it might be proper to deviate from "the book." With each unique lineup of players, you'll learn to "slant" your play for maintained effectiveness.

Finally, you must never stop learning—from books, from your own poker soul searching and from other players. You'll never know it all. Remember that every poker player, strong or weak knows something the other guy doesn't. Some

very useful tactical tidbits will come from the mouths of players you consider unfit to carry your chip rack. Keep your
mind open and absorb them all. You'll be a better player for
it.

Glossary

ante: in stud games, a small fee paid to the pot before being dealt the first three cards.

baby: a low card, usually between an Ace and a 5.

back door: a straight draw or flush draw that needs two consecutive cards to complete.

bad beat: losing with a hand that was well out in front earlier on.

big bet: the larger bet in any dual structure limit game, such as $80 in a $40/$80 game.

big blind: in flop style poker, the larger of the two mandatory bets prior to dealing the cards.

blank: a dealt card which appears to have no affect on the hand.

blind: in flop style poker, a mandatory bet posted prior to dealing the cards.

bluff: betting with a probable loser in an attempt the force an opponent to fold.

brick: in hi/lo poker, a 9 or higher which is dealt to an obvious low hand.

bring-in: in stud style poker, a small bet which the lowest card on 3rd Street must make.

buried pair: in stud style poker, a pair in the hole.

button: in flop style poker, a round disc which sits in front of the player in last position.

calling station: a player who seldom raises but almost always calls.

check/raise: the act of checking, then raising after someone else bets.

connectors: in Hold'em or Omaha, hole cards which run in numerical succession such as 8/9.

counterfeit: in Omaha, a low board card which ruins a player's low hand—usually an Ace or 2.

cowboy: a King.

crying call: when a player calls on the end expecting to find that he's beaten.

dead cards: played out cards that would have helped your hand.

dog: being more likely to lose the hand than win it.

door card: in stud style poker, a player's first up-card.

double gut-shot: a two way inside straight draw, such as having 7/8 when the board is 4-5-10-J.

draw: four parts to a straight or flush, such as having four spades or a 9/10/J/Q.

drawing dead: unable to win the hand even if you catch your best possible card.

draw-out: to come from behind and win the hand.

family pot: a pot in which nearly every player at the table is participating.

favorite: being more likely to win the hand than lose it.

flop: in Hold'em and Omaha, three cards turned up together in the center of the table.

free-roll: in hi/lo poker, having one side locked up while trying for the other end.

5th Street: the fifth card in stud games and the fifth board card in flop games.

4th Street: the fourth card in stud games and the fourth board card in flop games.

gut-shot: an inside straight draw such as 6/7/9/10.

heads up: playing alone with one other player.

hi/lo: split pot poker in which the highest and lowest hands divide the pot equally.

hogger: a hand that wins both ends of a hi/lo pot.

in the pocket: the cards a player has in the hole.

kicker: the highest card in your hand after considering your pair(s).

live card: a potentially helpful card that is still available.

loose: a player who plays a lot of hands rather than folds.

maniac: a recklessly aggressive player.

muck: to fold, discard or foul a card or a hand; also, the used cards.

multi-way: a pot which has more than two contestants.

nuts: the best possible hand considering the cards that are exposed.

offsuit: cards of different suits such as the King of clubs and the Queen of hearts in Hold'em.

open-end: a two-sided straight draw such as 7/8/9/10.

out(s): a card that will complete your hand, such as a spade to a 4-flush in spades.

overcard: having a card that is higher than an opponent's likely pair.

overlay: receiving higher pot odds than your odds against winning the pot.

overpair: having a higher pair than a key exposed card in the hand.

pocket pair: having a buried pair in the hole.

position: where you are located in the betting order of this particular hand.

pot odds: odds formed by dividing the cost of a call into the size of the pot.

quartered: in hi/lo poker, tying for either the high or the low—thereby receiving 1/4th of the pot.

Queens up: having two pair with a pair of Queens as the higher pair.

rag: in flop style poker, an apparently useless board card.

rainbow: in Hold'em or Omaha, a flop that contains three cards of different suits.

rake: the money collected by the house for running a poker game.

read: deducing an opponent's holding from information given during the hand.

release: the act of folding one's hand.

represent: to purport having a hand that you actually don't by playing deceptively.

re-route: to change directions in hi/lo poker, usually starting out low and finishing high.

river: the final card in any poker hand.

rock: a player who plays very few hands—folding most of the time.

rolled up: in stud poker, having three of a kind on the first three cards.

rough low: when the 2nd highest card in your low poker hand is just one rank below its highest.

runners: two exposed cards in numerical succession such as 8/9, or suited such as club, club.

rush: the phenomenon of catching one good hand after another—a streak.

scoop: to win both ends of a hi/lo pot.

second pair: in flop type games, pairing a hole card with the second highest card on board.

set: in flop type games, making trips with a pair in the hole and the trip card on board.

semi-bluff: to represent presently non-existent strength with a good chance of improving.

showdown: turning up the hole cards at the end of the hand.

sixthed: splitting either the high or low end of a hi/lo pot three ways, thereby getting only 1/6th.

6th Street: in stud type games, the sixth card.

skip-straight: in stud type games, a starting 3-straight with a gap such as 7/9/10.

small blind: in flop style poker, the smaller of the two mandatory bets prior to dealing the cards.

small bet: the smaller bet in any dual structure limit game, such as $40 in a $40/$80 game.

smooth low: when the second highest card in your low poker hand is at least two ranks below its highest.

split pair: in stud type games, starting with a pair having one pair card up and the other down.

stone cold bluff: bluffing with an absolutely hopeless hand.

street: referring to the stage of a poker hand—3rd Street is the third card, etc.

stuck: currently being a loser in this particular poker game.

suited: two or more cards of the same suit.

tell: inadvertent information given away by a player which reveals the strength of his hand.

3rd Street: in stud-type games, the first three cards.

tight: a player who plays very few hands—folding most of the time.

top pair: in flop type games, pairing one of your hole cards with the highest card on board.

trips: having any three of a kind in stud, or a pair on the board with the third buried in flop poker.

turn: the second up-card in stud games and the fourth board card in Hold'em or Omaha.

underpair: having a pair lower than the rank of a key exposed card in the hand.

unsuited: cards in one hand of different suits, such as the 9 of clubs and the 7 of hearts

wheel: in hi/lo poker, an Ace/2/3/4/5 which makes a perfect low as well as a 5 high straight.

Index